A NOTE ON THE AUTHOR

Kevin White was born in England and studied there at the University of Durham and in the United States at the Ohio State University, where he received a Ph.D. in American history. He has written widely on historical issues of sex and gender, including *The First Sexual Revolution: The Emergence of Male Heterosexuality in Modern America*. He is now a tutorial fellow at the University of Sussex.

ELISEO VIVAS

GARLAND BIBLIOGRAPHIES OF
MODERN CRITICS AND CRITICAL SCHOOLS
(General Editor: William E. Cain)
Vol. 1

GARLAND REFERENCE LIBRARY
OF THE HUMANITIES
Vol. 267

Garland Bibliographies of
Modern Critics and Critical Schools

GENERAL EDITOR:
William E. Cain (Wellesley College)

ELISEO VIVAS
An Annotated Bibliography

Hugh Mercer Curtler

GARLAND PUBLISHING, INC. • NEW YORK & LONDON
1982

Library of Congress Cataloging in Publication Data

Curtler, Hugh Mercer.
  Eliseo Vivas : an annotated bibliography.

  (Garland bibliographies of modern critics and
critical schools ; v. 1) (Garland reference library of
the humanities ; v. 267)
  Includes index.
  1. Vivas, Eliseo—Bibliography. I. Title. II. Series. III. Series: Garland reference library of the
humanities ; v. 267.
Z8944.32.C87 [PN75.V58]   016.809   82–921
ISBN 0–8240–9300–3   AACR2

Printed on acid-free, 250-year-life paper
Manufactured in the United States of America

GENERAL EDITOR'S INTRODUCTION

The Garland Bibliographies of Modern Critics and Critical Schools series is intended to provide bibliographic treatment of major critics and critical schools of the twentieth century. Each volume includes an introduction that surveys the critic's life, career, influence, and achievement, or, in the case of the volumes devoted to a critical school, presents an account of its central figures, origins, relation to other critical movements and trends, and the like.

Each volume is fully annotated and contains listings for both primary and secondary materials. The annotations are meant to be ample and detailed, in order to explain clearly, especially for a reader coming to a critic or critical school for the first time, the point and purpose of a book or essay. In this sense, the bibliographies are also designed to be critical guides. We hope that the volumes will inform and stimulate the reader even as they give basic information about what material exists and where it may be located.

We have tried to include as many of the most important critics and critical schools in this series as possible, but some have been omitted. Some critics and critical schools have already received (or are in the process of receiving) adequate treatment, and we see no need to duplicate the efforts of others.

WILLIAM E. CAIN
Wellesley College

CONTENTS

PREFACE

I would like to thank Eliseo Vivas for his invaluable assistance in providing me with a wealth of material required for this study, and for his help in reading the first draft of the manuscript.

In addition, I must acknowledge the groundwork laid by Alan Shields in his very fine bibliography at the end of *¡Viva Vivas!* which provided an excellent frame of reference for this study. Other people have made significant contributions as well. Carol Hirmer typed the drafts of the manuscript and Mary Jane Striegel of the Southwest State University library was tireless in providing information and source material. The general editor for this series, William Cain, has been patient and helpful throughout, and a research grant from Southwest State University made it possible to cover most of the expenses involved in preparing this manuscript. To all of these people I give my heartfelt thanks.

The careful reader will note that the information about some of Professor Vivas' very early essays is incomplete. This is unfortunate, but unavoidable in light of the date and type of work cited. This blemish should not deter the scholar or general reader interested in determining Eliseo Vivas' place in contemporary philosophy and criticism, however.

H.M.C.

INTRODUCTION

Eliseo Vivas was born of Venezuelan parents in Pamplona, Co-
lombia, on July 13, 1901. He came to the United States in 1915
and at the urging of his parents enrolled at the Brooklyn
Polytechnic Institute to work for a degree in engineering. By
chance he was placed in a freshman English class taught by
Joseph Wood Krutch in the Fall of 1919 and discovered that he
had both an aversion to engineering and a love of literature.
After several years of struggle with his parents and a couple of
years in Greenwich Village proving to himself that he did not
have whatever it takes to be a bohemian, he applied for and
obtained a Zona Gale scholarship to the University of Wisconsin where he took a degree in 1928. He received his Ph.D. in
philosophy in 1935 at Wisconsin and remained there as an As-
sistant Professor of Philosophy until 1944; he then went to the
University of Chicago as an Associate Professor of Philosophy
for one year and then to Ohio State University where he held a
joint Professorship in English and Philosophy until 1951. At
that point he accepted the John Evans Chair of Moral and
Intellectual Philosophy at Northwestern University, where he
remained until his retirement in 1969. He has had a variety of
Visiting Professorships at such institutions as Brooklyn College,
Columbia University, the University of Illinois, the University
of North Carolina, the University of Puerto Rico, and the University of Mexico. He was Larwill Lecturer at Kenyon College
in 1940, Mahlon Powell Lecturer at Indiana University in 1952,
and Visiting Professor of English at the University of Iowa
from 1966 until 1968. After his retirement from Northwestern
University he was Distinguished Visiting Professor at Rockford
College for two years.

Vivas is currently Emeritus Professor of Philosophy at
Northwestern University and lives with his wife, Dorothy, in

Wilmette, Illinois. He serves on the editorial boards of both *Modern Age* and *The Intercollegiate Review*, and in 1976 saw a Festschrift entitled *¡Viva Vivas!* published in honor of his 75th birthday. This was followed in the Spring of 1979 by his election as one of only four Honorary Members of the Philadelphia Society.

During his philosophical journey Vivas has managed to travel comfortably with both poets and philosophers, even though the company in one camp is frequently antagonistic to its "rivals" in the other, and although there is often a language barrier between the two. Vivas is a philosopher who has a deep and abiding love of literature, or "poetry" as he prefers to call it. By reading such poets as D.H. Lawrence, he learned to write with a rich prose style, which alone is sufficient to set him apart from most contemporary academics. He is a man of "styled thought," a philosopher who has made important contributions to both philosophy and criticism in a style that "stings and celebrates," to quote a long-time friend and colleague, William Earle. Vivas was at the center of the movement known as "the New Criticism," a movement led by John Crowe Ransom and including such thinkers as Cleanth Brooks, Allen Tate, and Robert Penn Warren, and had the distinction of being called "the aesthetician of the group" by his critic Walter Sutton.[1]

Professor Sutton's label is quite apt, of course, in that it points to two important truths: (1) Vivas is one of the few critics, new or old, who has bothered to develop a complete aesthetic, and (2) Vivas has been one of the preeminent thinkers among the "new critics." Additionally, his aesthetics informs his criticism at every turn, and it is here that we must begin in order to understand Vivas' theory of criticism. As we do so we should focus attention on those features of special interest to students of literature and try, at the same time, to see precisely how the aesthetics of Eliseo Vivas provides the basis for his criticism. Toward that end we shall concentrate for the most part on Vivas' book-length study of D.H. Lawrence.

To begin with, the functions of criticism, according to Vivas, are "to guide and improve public taste, to disclose the relations of art, considered purely as art, to non-aesthetic activities and values, to determine the comparative worth of the aesthetic qualities embodied in objects which may compete for our attention, and to enlighten the artist on the true nature and meaning of his created object, since the artist may do better or worse or quite differently than he intends to."[2]

When one engages a literary work of art fully and "intransitively," criticism is forgotten. But criticism makes it *possible* for the spectator to engage the "poem" fully, to "go it alone with the poem, in the hope of getting his reward for his efforts—the opportunity to live for a moment in the universe that is the aesthetic object."[3] Criticism does this because its primary purpose is to elucidate the meanings and values the critic finds residing in the poem. These values are not created by the poet, however, since they subsist independently of the poet and his poem: they have independent "status in being" and are discovered by the poet in the process of creating his work of art. The poet's activity, properly understood, is a "creative discovery." To grasp this fully, we must first discuss the question of what values are for an "axiological realist," one who insists that values are real since they have "status in being."

Briefly put, values are aspects or qualities of our intersubjective world, "gestalt" qualities in the language of Wolfgang Köhler. Of these qualities it has been said that they "make their appearance in art more often and more strikingly than anywhere else and are regarded by many authorities as the very essence of the appeal and tenacious hold art has had at all times and in all places. The music of Beethoven is often powerful and even titanic, although as in the case of Michaelangelo's sculpture there are many examples of gentle tenderness; the faces of Renaissance madonnas are wistful and sad; the music of Mozart frequently is melancholy in spite of the gaiety of its surface; the glass of Chartres glistens with radiant color; many passages of Reger fairly burst with romantic fervor, etc."[4] We must note, however, that though their presence there is more striking, values are not only found in art, but in the people, objects, and events that surround us; they comprise parts of our experience and they comprise vital parts of our moral experience. We give names to these gestalt qualities—as we do in art—to connote the aspect or feature of an event, say, that commands our approval: we find it valuable, not because we want to or because we find it pleasant to do so—though this may be the case—but because a response to that quality is *re-quired*. Values, as Vivas insists, have "requiredness." We say of a young man who pulls a child from in front of a speeding car, "he is brave," and "bravery" is as much a *part* of that event as the frantic movements, the cries of the child, the screech of the wheels, and the look of terror in the young man's eyes.

The poet invites us to look at our world again through his work, and if he has created a work of art, there is more *there* than mere personal statement. And when we return to our world we find more there than we had seen before. This "more" that is "there" we call "value," and it comprises a part of the warp and woof of human experience, though we often have difficulty finding it through the fog of indifference, indolence, bias, insensitivity, and self-centeredness that characterizes "human nature."

Of the poet's creative discovery, Vivas has said that

> [the poet] tears the horny cataract of conceptual abstrac-
> tions from the soul's eyes, the worn-out categories, the
> stereotyped modes of response to the world, the brittle
> formulas. In their place he gives us fresh, quick, tender,
> unmediated revelations of the world of nature and man.
> Having freed us from our "ideas" he substitutes his own
> freshly organized experience, through which we are able to
> understand aesthetically, to grasp by immediate apprehen-
> sion, those aspects of contemporary experience that without
> his aid would remain threatening and oppressive because
> they would remain chaotic. The poet's organization consti-
> tutes a discovery, but one that is creative. . . . The lenses he
> offers us we use as a fresh and adequate categorical scheme,
> by which we grasp the world anew; with it we now sense
> what he sensed, and when we respond properly to his work
> we use it later, much later, to judge as best we may what he
> sensed and grasped—*later*, for during the time we are in
> intimate relationship to his work, if we know how to re-
> spond to it, all we do is behold. Without these lenses,
> purblind, we would stumble in the dark, not realizing the
> true shape of things.[5]

Because of the lofty perch on which Vivas places the poet's creation and because of the seriousness with which Vivas takes poetry, he repeatedly insists that we look to the poem if we want to discover what the poet meant. As for the poet, "he is a dribbling liar."[6] Herein lies the heart of Vivas' "contextualist" criticism, a criticism that considers biographical information about the author, historical background, interest in the artist's neurosis, the number of his mistresses, and the amount of time he spent in poverty largely irrelevant. The work of art is "autotelic" and it must stand on its own two aesthetic feet: it obeys its own laws and canons which render external considerations extraneous. "In a novel a man may have as large a harem as he happens to have and that is the end of the matter and a church may be as dead as it happens to be and that too is the end of the matter."[7]

The substance of the poem must be distinguished from the subject matter, and the former cannot be reduced to the latter without leaving a residue. The subject matter is in-formed by the artist and the result is the substance of art, that which is *sui generis* and can only be met on its own ground in what Vivas calls "rapt, intransitive attention." It is the artist's activity of "informing" and "transubstancing" the subject matter of ordinary experience that gives the work its artistic value. "Something happens to the experience that goes into art—the matter for art—before it becomes the substance of art. . . . The change, of course, is the result of the creative process, and is complete in so far as the artist is able to bring creative energy into its consummation and is not distracted by any other motive than that of creating an object that elicits an aesthetic response."[8] In this regard, *Aaron's Rod*, for example, fails as art because "the values [of the man Lawrence] have spilled over into the art without having been subjected to the process of informing and transubstancing, and the result is that the work is turbid; [Lawrence's personal values and convictions] are there making themselves felt by their conspicuous presence. . . ."[9]

Vivas is emphatic in his insistence that we separate the artist from the person in the same way that we separate substance from subject matter. As he shows, Dostoevsky the poet is not the same person as Dostoevsky the man. The one is a genius, a poet "in spite of himself," while the other was an epileptic, a

compulsive gambler, a political prisoner, and a romantic conservative who saw Russia's hope in the peasants and their sim-
ple faith. The two are not one by any means.[10] Likewise, the
subject matter of Dostoevsky's poems (or novels, if you will) is
found in the notebooks that he left behind. This point might
become clearer if we pursue a concrete case.

In Dostoevsky's notebooks we read about the poet's "idea"
for *Crime and Punishment*. This "idea" leads him to the following
prediction in a letter he wrote to his publisher prior to complet-
ing his manuscript:

> The idea of the story . . . is a psychological account of a
> crime. A young man expelled from the University, a
> bourgeois by origin and living in extreme poverty, light-
> hearted, unstable in his ideas, has surrendered to several
> strange, "unfinished" ideas which are in the air. He decided
> to get out of his bad position at a stroke. He decided to kill
> an old woman . . . to rob her, in order to make happy his
> mother, who lives in a provincial district, to rescue a sister
> . . . to finish his studies, go abroad, and then be honest the
> rest of his life. . . .
>
> He spends almost a month after [his crime] until the
> final catastrophe; almost no suspicions existed or could exist
> against him. There, too, the psychological process of crime
> develops. Insoluble problems arise for the murderer; un-
> suspected and unexpected feelings torment his heart. The
> truth of God and the law of the earth take their toll, and he
> ends by being forced to denounce himself, forced even if he
> should perish in jail, to rejoin people . . . the criminal him-
> self decides to accept torments in order to redeem his act.[11]

Clearly, we would have to question a number of aspects of
Dostoevsky's version of his "idea" when it is set against a background of the novel itself. First, it is not at all clear *why* Raskol-
nikov killed the old woman. Indeed, it is a central question for
interpreters of the novel, and can hardly be handled as simply
as the author himself handles it. Second, the sequence of
events changed between the formulation of the author's "idea"
and the execution of that idea in the writing of the novel. Ras-
kolnikov confesses at the urging of Sonya and as a result of the
shock of Svidrigialov's suicide—not for the reasons given by the
author. One might argue that Dostoevsky's unerring poetic

honesty made him respond to the constraints placed on him by the poem itself, and he had to abandon his "idea." In Vivas' terms, what has happened up to the end of the novel proper is that the subject matter of the poem has become the substance of the poem, and in the process the poet has responded to the demands of the work as he wrote it. When he finished, however, he discovered that he had not made his "point." Thus the epilogue became philosophically necessary, though it is poetically flawed. This is one of the few cases where Dostoevsky the man got the better of Dostoevsky the poet. Clearly, it was important to the man that his hero exhibit "unexpected feelings . . . the truth of God and the law of the earth," so important that the poet lost control of the poem.

Now whether or not one accepts this analysis of *Crime and Punishment*, it should be clear that the critic armed with Vivas' theoretical equipment can indeed "enlighten the artist on the true nature and meaning of his created object." In general, the autotelic nature of the poem makes it obey its own rules and strictures, and any attempt to hammer home a philosophical or theological "point" strikes the intent spectator as dishonest, an intrusion into the work of factors that ought to lie outside and remain there. It is a violation of the canons of aesthetic "truth," in the only sense of this term that Vivas will allow, since the poet is not concerned with truth or with "knowledge" in any straightforward sense.

This point has bothered a number of Vivas' critics because, among other things, it seems to raise questions about the legitimacy of literary criticism. The issue focuses on Vivas' important distinction between the "residential" and the "non-residential" functions of the poem.

Bear in mind that for Vivas the poem is first and foremost a work of art—which is why he prefers the term "poetry" to the more common term "literature." As a result, the work must be confronted directly in an aesthetic response that is intransitive, which is to say, it is primarily imaginative, prereflexive, and rich with feeling. To be sure, the act of intransitive attention is preceded by analysis—for this is the job of the critic—but this simply prepares the spectator for a fuller, richer, more engrossing experience. The spectator who engages the work fully as

art, as a self-sufficient whole, does not think about the work—
that comes later. Initially one's response is one of ecstasy, a
coming out of oneself, a "transaction" between the spectator
and the object that actually creates the work of art as an object-
for-a-subject, an object that has being for only as long as the
subject (the spectator) engages the work in rapt, intransitive
attention. We shall see later how these idealistic claims meld
with the realistic elements of Vivas' metaphysics. At this point,
it is only necessary to be clear that art, *in se*, cannot be said to
yield knowledge without "stretching the coefficient of elasticity
of language."

Properly speaking, we do not read poetry to discover
philosophical, sociological, psychological, or anthropological
ideas:

> The critic who is interested in going through literature to
> moral philosophy, political thought, social theory, or the
> rest, is a man the seriousness of whose interest in any of
> these disciplines can be questioned. As a moral philosopher,
> no novelist or literary critic can tie Kant's shoes or those of
> Bishop Butler; I know of no novelist or literary critic who as
> a political thinker can hold a candle to Edmund Burke or
> Michael Oakeshott, or who as a sociologist can rival Karl
> Marx or Max Weber. A literary critic who thinks he can go
> through literature to a well-established discipline cultivated
> by the men I mentioned or others of lesser stature is a
> dilettante in the pejorative sense of that term. He can't take
> his drink at the bar and take it straight; he sits in a booth
> and sweetens his bourbon with ginger ale or, God forbid,
> with coca-cola.[12]

Note the careful selection of terms in this passage. The poet
does not produce "a well-established discipline." The poet does
not, *qua* poet, provide us with discursive, systematic knowledge.
Instead he provides food for thought, fragments, bits and
pieces, insights, and occasionally, perhaps, profound
observations. The poet sees more deeply and conveys more
vividly *precisely because* he is unencumbered by conceptual bag-
gage. Imagination is closer to lived experience than is concep-
tualization, and the language of the poet is rich with metaphor
and image and as such holds us closer to lived experience than
we can be when we stop to think *about* the experience. This is

not to say that poetry is mindless or thoughtless, only that it employs different functions, or, as they were once called, "faculties," of the mind. The poet purchases vivid depiction and immediacy at the price of systematic wholeness. But it is a price worth paying because the poet provides us with values and meanings that we would otherwise be without: our world would otherwise be unknowable, which is to say, impossible. To be precise, the poet is creator of culture, which is comprised of art, religion, cognition, and morality, the four basic symbolic activities of the human mind, according to Vivas. Adopting, and adapting, the notion of symbol from Cassirer, Vivas developed it in a systematic way, placing much greater stress on poetry as the *sine qua non* of culture: without the language, the schema, and the categories supplied by the poet we would not have a world at all; cognition, religion, and morality would not be possible.[13]

The differences between poetry and philosophy do not entail the claim that one is superior to the other: only that they are not alike. Because they are different we need them both—those of us who seek lamely to make sense out of our world. And because they are different what is appropriate to philosophy is inappropriate to poetry and *vice versa*, as we saw with the epilogue to *Crime and Punishment*. One of the major functions of the critic, therefore, is that of "distinguishing poetry from prophecy, art from message; aesthetic vision authentically revealed from propaganda; the world he discovered in and through the act of creation from [a poet's] criticism and turbid lucubrations. The created world will be found at its best to be a powerful aesthetic organization of values and disvalues, the matter of experience as grasped by a gifted mind and transmuted and informed by it."[14] In the case of *Kangaroo*, for example, Vivas notes that when Richard Somers reflects that " 'the human heart must have an absolute. It is one of the conditions of being human. The only thing is the God of all passion . . .,' we get a very definite sense that not only did Richard Lovat Somers know it, but that Lawrence wanted us to know it; and he wanted us to know it not in order to know Richard but for its own sake, because he wants us to accept it. And here is the difference between art and message."[15]

What this means is that criticism is not only a legitimate

activity, it is a necessary activity if we are to make sense out of what the poet has delivered into our hands. In addition, after the explanations of the critic the spectator is better able to enter into the work of art as a result of the increased sophistication and sensitivity that results from critical studies.

We must, however, face the problem deferred above: how do the idealistic tenets of Vivas' aesthetic blend with the realistic elements of his metaphysics? How does the view that we *constitute* the work of art in the mental act of transaction with the poem as it appears in the printed or the spoken word blend with the view that real, objective values are to be discovered in and through the work of art? The answer lies in Vivas' notion of the "constitutive symbol"—clearly one of the most distinctive contributions he has made to the theory of criticism.

A lengthy discussion of the constitutive symbol appears at the end of Vivas' study of the writings of D.H. Lawrence. In the appendix to that work, he quotes Lawrence himself with approval:

> You can't give a great symbol a 'meaning'. Symbols are organic units of consciousness with a life of their own, and you can never explain them away, because their value is dynamic, emotional, belonging to the sense-consciousness of the body and the soul, and not simply mental. An allegorical image has a *meaning*. Mr. Facing-both-ways has a meaning. But I defy you to lay your finger on Janus, who is a symbol.[16]

The novel as a work of art contains within it a variety of symbols. These are concrete embodiments of objective, real values that have status in being independent of the poet or his poem. These symbols are concrete universals, in Hegel's sense of this term, that is, they are *both* concrete and universal, concrete in that they denote a specific entity within the poem itself, and universal in their reference to something outside the poem, aspects of our common human experience that we had previously ignored. Father Zossima, in *The Brothers Karamazov*, is a constitutive symbol in that he is who he is in the novel, a concrete character of flesh and bones, while at the same time (though in another respect) he signifies the values of humility, abject self-denial, and a relentless love of his fellow man. For

Vivas these symbols are constitutive because they constitute the ultimate value and substance of the poem. But the adjective "constitutive" is used in more than one sense.

Precisely because the poem is constituted by the mind, insofar as the poem is a work of art, and insofar as it contains within it symbols that refer beyond the poem to something *else*, the various components of the poem can be regarded as phenomenal, or ideal, and at the same time, though in another respect, real and valuable. These values that are revealed in and through the language of the poem come later on to reside in our culture and, indeed, as we saw above, to constitute that culture; or they were in culture but were ignored before the poet took note of them and drew them to our attention. Thus, the symbols are "constitutive" in this regard as well. In Lawrence's stories, for example, "the doll, the fox, the rocking horse, are in the last analysis beyond elucidation by discursive language. They are constitutive symbols." [17] To say that they are "beyond discursive language" is to stress their particularity, as does Lawrence, and their intimate relationship to the substance of the poem, of which they constitute essential elements. Thus these symbols are constitutive from the point of view of the poem itself, and this is another sense of the adjective. In addition, as we have noted, the values and meanings that are found in and through the language of the poem come to constitute the culture within which they are written. It is in this sense that Vivas insists that "it is truer to say that the world imitates the novel than to say that the novel imitates the world." [18] The poet is "creator of culture" and provides us with the lenses through which we come to know our world better. Vivas' claim finds an echo, interestingly, in the writings of Marcel Proust. One rather long comment by Proust is especially revealing:

> People of taste and refinement tell us nowadays that Renoir is one of the greatest painters of the last century. But in so saying they forget the element of Time, and it took a great deal of time, well into the present century, before Renoir was hailed as a great artist. To succeed thus in gaining recognition, the original painter, the original writer, proceeds along lines adopted by oculists. The course of treatment they give us by their painting or by their prose is not always

agreeable to us. When it is at an end the operator says to us:
'Now look!' And, lo and behold, the world around us (which
was not created once and for all, but is created afresh as
often as an original artist is born) appears to us entirely
different from the old world, but perfectly clear. Women
pass in the street, different from what they used to be,
because they are Renoirs, those Renoir types which we per-
sistently refused to see as women. . . . Such is the new and
perishable universe which has just been created. It will last
until the next geological catastrophe is precipitated by a
new painter or a writer of original talent.[19]

Because life imitates art in the sense that the world as we
know it is constituted by the categories and schemata supplied
by the poets, the place of the poet in culture is central in Vivas'
view. This fact, together with his commitment to the view that
values and disvalues are real, objective aspects of our human
world, has led Vivas to a careful scrutiny of American culture
over the years. Accordingly, he has struggled against what he
considers to be the destructive influences of both liberalism (a
liberalism he once espoused) and scientism, or the view that the
exact sciences provide the prototype of a method that must be
employed if man himself is to be made an object of knowledge.

His struggle has been set against a background of his
axiological realism, the view that values have "ontic" status, or
are objective, real properties of our common world.

This view has been ridiculed in this century as being unduly
complex and replete with "unverifiable" propositions. But we
must beware when we hack and hew with Occam's razor that we
not sever an artery. In Vivas' considered opinion, this is precisely what has been done, and he would agree with Robert
Hutchins when he regretted that "everything we value is now
value free." Vivas has argued with great force that there is
something wrong with our spectacles, not with our world.
Value still comprises a part of our world, but we seek to reduce
it to "emotion," "desire," "interest," or "opinion." Speaking in
the past tense, Vivas has said, "one thing was clear [to his alter-
ego Alonzo Quijano] . . . the basic assumption of naturalists to
the effect that the universe was value free was not a self-evident
truth, but a metaphysical assumption that could be chal-

lenged."[20] Indeed, as Vivas has shown repeatedly, the claims of the naturalists are based quite frequently on "metaphysical assumptions," or articles of faith, despite the insistence of the naturalists themselves upon clinical methods and antiseptic procedures devoid of any taint of metaphysics. This applies to the Freudian account of the origin of conscience no less than the hedonism of Marcuse, to the "missing link" of the anthropologists no less than Darwin's hypothesis about the descent of man. Naturalism in its various manifestations forms a type of reductionism that would decapitate phenomena to fit the Procrustean bed of its methods rather than alter procedures or question assumptions to fully explain complex phenomena. Thus it is *inadequate* as it stands if we are to try to understand human experience *as it is*, and not as we choose to find it. It is in this sense that Vivas insists that he is an "empiricist" who has greater concern for the world as he finds it than the neo-positivists and scientistic naturalists who ignore aspects of experience if they cannot render an account of them in their pre-selected idiom. Their obduracy in this regard amounts to what Vivas calls an "aprioristic methodolatry" of the worst sort, a metaphysical commitment by the haters of metaphysics that is all the more vicious because it is never questioned.

One of the major flaws of naturalism, as Vivas perceives it, is that it totally neglects the tragic dimension of human experience. Vivas' concern for tragedy has occupied him throughout his academic career and it provides a bridge between his aesthetics and criticism and his philosophy of culture and conservatism. It would thus seem worthwhile to take a brief look at what Vivas calls "unmitigated" tragedy.

Vivas is convinced that unmitigated tragedy reveals that our world is flawed. That is to say, when we reflect on the meanings and values in a play such as *King Lear*, we are confronted by a tragic vision that reveals inexplicable evil. The death of Cordelia, for example, and the extraordinary behavior of the "pelican daughters," cannot be explained away in terms of a higher moral order, because they are totally gratuitous, symptomatic of the fact that we are indeed poor forked animals "as flies to wanton boys," and helpless in the face of fatal mistakes on a cosmic scale. At the end of the play the tensions that have held us throughout are still unresolved, and we are left dismayed and dissatisfied, and our eyes are opened to a new and terrifying dimension of human existence. The tragedy of Cordelia is totally undeserved—by her, to be sure, and by Lear as well since he has already been thoroughly punished even before she dies at the end of the play. Vivas' response is not unlike that of Ivan Karamazov, who informs his brother Alyosha that he cannot accept the suffering of innocent children, and that in the face of that suffering he "gives Him back his ticket." The suffering is not *deserved* and is therefore "unmitigated." If we, with Vivas,

> turn attentively to the range of experience that we can discern through the lenses offered us by the tragic poet, we see more than we saw before, and what we see has a different hue. We men of today, and not men of the nineteenth century living today, we who have assimilated what Dostoevsky and Kafka have taught us to see, what Nietzsche and Freud have disclosed, have seen through the lie of meliorism and the delusions of scientism. We the dupes of betrayed hopes, the men of lost faith, the victims of relentless terror, we left meliorism and scientism behind long ago. Our problem is not that of satisfying our cravings or negotiating our rights. Men have always known how to take frustration in their stride. And in this respect we are no lesser men than our ancestors. To see tragedy as the frustration of desire or the conflict of interest is the privilege—a privilege I do not envy him—of the worshipper of Sovereign Reason. Ours is a different age. What we may call the Baconian lie has been exposed.[21]

But few of us are aware that the Baconian lie has been exposed. We are, as a culture, blind to many of the truths and values that surround us just as we are to the tragic dimension that is equally real. These convictions came to Vivas gradually as he wrestled with naturalism and a liberalism that worshipped scientific Progress. Always, it was to the poets that Vivas listened with rapt attention, and it was to poetry that he returned again and again. The poets insist that the world is not only flawed, they insist that ours is a spiteful age, one that is "instinct with hatred of values."

> ... the evidence ... is to be gathered by anyone who

chooses to look into the texture of our Western culture, as
expressed in much of our poetry and painting, no less than
in our philosophy, for our higher activities are instinct with
self-hatred. It is to be found in Proust, in D.H. Lawrence, in
Céline, in Paul Bowles, in Henry Miller, just as it can be
found in the positivistic and analytic desire to debunk our
belief in value and deny the objectivity of the structures
which maintain culture. . . .[22]

Note here that the reality of values and the presence of iniquity
are not denied; they are only ignored at the cost of a blindness
that "has beaten the universe into a sheet and made of it a
surface, a mere appearance. When we look for reality we
search for appearance."[23] These words of Ortega y Gasset reflect the same concerns that have given rise to Vivas' conservatism, since it is to the restoration of wholeness of vision that
Vivas' conservatism speaks, and it is his concern for value, the
cornerstone of his philosophical position, that led him from
liberalism to conservatism.

Unfortunately, Vivas' conservatism has placed him in dis-
favor with many of his colleagues, who equate it with no-
mindedness. Furthermore, because of his advocacy of axiological realism, Vivas has found himself defending a philosophical
position that is considered anachronistic by many American
and British philosophers. Note here, however, that the issue is
the manner in which the man chooses to do philosophy and
not, as it should be, the question of whether his philosophical
view is more or less adequate to human experience.

Fascinating and rich though it is, however, we must admit
that Vivas' theory of criticism and his aesthetics are not without
problems and that Vivas has not had the influence he deserves.
In bringing this Introduction to a close, then, we must confront
these concerns and seek a balanced perspective. Thus, even
though in doing so we become involved in some speculation
about probable causes, we must discuss the question of Vivas'
influence on his contemporaries and then turn to one or two of
the problems that readers have had with his philosophical system as it concerns his aesthetics.

Anyone who seeks an overview of Vivas' position confronts
a practical difficulty that must be weighed when one considers

the question of the man's influence. His work is vast and spread out over a long period of time and in a great many periodicals and journals. While his first collection of essays, which he called *Creation and Discovery*, contains some of his critical essays, it nonetheless contains less than half of his work in this area. Furthermore, his *D.H. Lawrence: The Failure and Triumph of Art* is the only book-length critical study he has provided thus far. His reputation as a major American critic, therefore, rests almost totally on these two books, despite their incompleteness.

Beyond this consideration, one must admit that Vivas has suffered by refusing to play certain academic games that one must play if one is to become a successful "careerist" (to use his term). Vivas has never sought to be fashionable, at least not since his break with naturalism in the late 1930's and early 1940's, and one will not find in his pocket a membership card for any "official" fraternity of professional philosophers. Further, he has been outspoken in his contempt for naturalism and other "orthodox" philosophies in a highly charged style that often ignores accepted forms of display. Some have found this refusal to play by their rules offensive. Others find it refreshing. But before we fall into the abyss of idle speculation about why others have not given Vivas his due, let us confess that some of the things he has said are not without difficulty, even to a sympathetic reader, and it is quite possible that this difficulty has militated against widespread acceptance of his views.

As was pointed out above, there is an apparent inconsistency between Vivas' phenomenalism and his axiological realism. As noted, this reader finds in Vivas' notion of the "constitutive symbol" a way out of that difficulty. But there remains a problem with his phenomenalism itself. Specifically, what is the relation between the spectator and the art object? What does it mean to say that the spectator views the poem "intransitively"? How is that possible?

Vivas has spoken to this problem repeatedly, and has sought, by means of his distinction between the "residential" and the "non-residential" aspects of the work of art, to answer those critics who have denied that art *can* be viewed "intransitively."[24] That is to say, Vivas grants his critics the point that literature refers in some way to the world of things, actions, and people; but its primary function is prereflexive. The poem must be grasped in the first instance in its "full presentational immediacy," as a work of art, before we are aware of its reference to something beyond itself. He even goes so far as to admit that reflective thought, in the form of criticism, helps to deepen and intensify this experience. But the aesthetic act is just that: an act in which one comes into direct contact with the felt quality of life itself, insofar as it is possible for a person to do that at all.

In his response to Walter Sutton, for example, Vivas points out that the poem enables a person to "grasp reality itself," and this act precedes any reference language might have to reality later on.[25] That is to say, the aesthetic act is primary and the referential act, which is reflective, is secondary or derivative. The mind constitutes reality in a synthetic act of the imagination, and any reference language has to reality must come later. This is not a new idea for one who had read his Kant carefully. But for Vivas the elements that make the synthesis possible are supplied, for the most part, by the poets. This means that Vivas takes Cassirer one step further away from Kant—though the fundamental insight remains Kantian to the core—by insisting that while the categories of the human understanding do indeed constitute the objective world, they are by no means fixed in four neat groups of three. Rather, they are fluid and are supplied in the first place by the poets who discover them creatively in the act of writing poems. From the point of view of the spectator, not to mention the poet himself, there can be no denying the genuine novelty of the poet's creation, since it is a novelty that makes our world anew. As Vivas has somewhere said, no one can read Dostoevsky and look at his fellow human beings in precisely the same way again.

The fact that the intransitivity of the aesthetic response is difficult to allow in the case of the poet who must use a language heavy with referential meaning implies only that genuine aesthetic responses are rare in the case of poetry; it does not mean that they are impossible. But this remains a problem for many who read Vivas. One of the better-known attacks on Vivas' notion of the aesthetic attitude, and on "attitude theorists" generally, is that of George Dickie, who argues that there is no distinctive aesthetic attitude and that viewing art "correctly" is simply a matter of paying attention.[26]

While Dickie's argument has some initial force, one must admit on reflection that he has ignored a fundamental fact of human consciousness, highly touted by phenomenologists, that consciousness is intentional. Dickie denies that aesthetic consciousness differs from any other consciousness because he cannot find any qualities peculiar to it—but he ignores the object of the aesthetic attitude. One thinks here of Clive Bell's "significant form" or Vivas' notion of "meanings and values," but the important point is that the aesthetic attitude is "intransitive attention" to a particular sort of object—or an object viewed a particular way. What one attends to at the moment of "rapt intransitive attention" is the surface of the object. The experience itself is primarily (exclusively?) imaginative and affective. It is not simply a question of paying attention, but of a particular sort of (imaginative/affective) absorption in a particular sort of object (art object or natural object viewed aesthetically—which is to say from the perspective of the "felt-quality" of the surface of the object).

Dickie's points that attitude theorists confuse the role of the critic and incorrectly remove morality from art do not really touch Vivas' analysis because of his distinction between the residential and the non-residential aspects of art. Residentially, criticism and morality have no place: they are not included among the aspects of the object viewed as *art*. From the non-residential perspective, however, one must allow room for criticism and admit that the moral dimensions of a novel (to use Dickie's example) are central. Dickie insists that criticism can be a part of aesthetic apprehension, but this is doubtful. It is more likely that criticism, which involves reflection and deliberation, occurs and is, or is not, followed by increased awareness of the aesthetic qualities of the object. These are, as I have tried to show in my exposition above, two discrete moments in the spectator's response to the object. They occur separately and can only interfere with one another if they overlap.

We should recall, though, that the intransitivity of the aesthetic response gives rise to Vivas' view that literature does not yield knowledge. This is not a view that is widely accepted, but at the risk of psychoanalyzing the opposition, one can understand the reticence of critics to accept a view that seems to raise basic questions about the legitimacy of their activities. A careful reading of what Vivas has said on the subject should allay these fears, however, since poetry plays such a critical role in Vivas' notion of what comprises "culture." But if one does not accept that view of the role of poetry, or literature, then its seriousness, and *pari passu* the legitimacy of criticism, is in doubt. It is easier to insist that literature does yield knowledge, even though in the end one must admit that it is a peculiar sort of knowledge indeed.

There can be little doubt that there are other aspects of Vivas' thought that have proven difficult for the modern, toothless mind, fed as it has been on the thin anti-metaphysical gruel of positivism.[27] But if one is willing to make it, the effort at comprehending Vivas' system is well worthwhile. His aesthetic arises out of his metaphysics and his critical theory rests comfortably within his aesthetics. And this complex interrelationship marks Vivas as a distinctive thinker among twentieth-century American philosophers and isolates him from other American critics as well. That he has managed to remain faithful to the demands of his systematic requirements while at the same time providing sensitive and insightful readings of the poems he takes seriously marks Eliseo Vivas as a philosopher and a critic of major stature.

NOTES

1. *The Artistic Transaction and Essays on the Theory of Literature*, p. 172. (Below, A4; cited as *AT* hereafter in notes.)

2. *Creation and Discovery*, p. 191. (Below, A2; cited as *C&D* hereafter in notes.)

3. *AT*, p. 198.

4. Introduction by Carroll C. Pratt to Köhler's *The Task of Gestalt Psychology* (Princeton: Princeton University Press, 1969), p. 10.

5. *D.H. Lawrence: The Failure and Triumph of Art*, p. x. (Below, A3; cited as *FTA* hereafter in notes.)

6. D.H. Lawrence, "The Novel," *Reflections on the Death of a Porcupine and Other Essays* (Philadelphia: Centaur Press, 1925).

7. *FTA*, p. 84.

8. *FTA*, p. 143.

9. *FTA*, p. 28. Also see pp. 61 and 69.

10. "Dostoevsky, 'Poet' in Spite of Himself," below, C124.

11. Quoted in the Norton Critical Edition of *Crime and Punishment*, tr. Coulson (New York: W.W. Norton and Co., 1964), p. 539.

12. Vivas, "Critical Assizes," below, C128.

13. *AT*, pp. 10 ff.

14. *FTA*, p. 5.

15. *FTA*, p. 60.

16. *FTA*, p. 274.

17. *FTA*, p. 281.

18. *FTA*, p. 285.

19. Proust, *Remembrance of Things Past*, tr. Scott Montcrieff (New York: Random House, 1932), Volume I, p. 950.

20. *Two Roads to Ignorance: A Quasi Biography*, p. 241. (Below, A6).

21. *AT*, p. 137.

22. *C&D*, p. 291, n. 10.

23. José Ortega y Gasset, *Meditations on Quixote*, tr. Evelyn Rugg (New York: W.W. Norton, Inc., 1961), p. 124.

24. See below, G38, for example.

25. Vivas, "Contextualism Reconsidered," below, C81.

26. George Dickie, "The Myth of the Aesthetic Attitude," below, G11.

27. Reference here is to such writers as Sidney Hook (see below, G20) and others of the species *logophilia*.

Part I
Primary Sources

A

BOOKS AND COLLECTIONS OF ESSAYS

A1 *The Moral Life and the Ethical Life.* Chicago: University of Chicago Press, 1950. xiv + 390 pp.

Introduction: Moral Philosophy Is a "Practical Science." Part I. "Animadversions Upon Naturalistic Moral Philosophies"; Ch. I, Mores and Morals; Ch. II, The Interest Theory I; Ch. III, The Interest Theory II; Ch. IV, The Interest Theory III; Ch. V, The Postulational Theory of Morality; Ch. VI, The Instrumentalist Moral Theory I; Ch. VII, The Instrumentalist Moral Theory II; Ch. VIII, The Instrumentalist Moral Theory III; Ch. IX, The Freudian Theory of Conscience; Ch. X, A Postscript; Ch. XI, Summary. Part II. "The Moral Life"; Ch. XII, The Resolution of a Moral Perplexity I; Ch. XIII, The Resolution of a Moral Perplexity II; Ch. XIV, The Resolution of a Moral Perplexity III; Ch. XV, The Ground and Source of Moral Authority; Ch. XVI, The Justification of a Moral Decision. Part III. "The Ethical Life"; Ch. XVII, The Discovery of the Ethical I; Ch. XVIII, The Discovery of the Ethical II; Ch. XIX, The Discovery of the Ethical III; Ch. XX, The Primacy of the Person.

Establishes the "axiological realism" that provides the cornerstone of Vivas' philosophical system. Begins by arguing that values are objective, real properties of external objects, and have "status in being." Part I is devoted to a critique of alternative theories--the "interest" theory, the "postulational" theory, and the "instrumentalist" theory of morality. These are "subjectivistic," reduce value to personal feeling or attitude, and therefore render it impossible to "resolve moral perplexities morally."

Develops Vivas' important essay "Animadversions on Naturalistic Ethics," first published in *Ethics* in April, 1946 (C49), and marks Vivas' break with the naturalism of John Dewey and his adoption of a Hartmannian realism with such interesting modifications as the radical demarkation

3

he makes between the "moral life" and the "ethical life."
Movement from the "moral" to the "ethical" arises as a result of one's acknowledgment of iniquity, either through
direct or vicarious experience. Recognition of genuine
iniquity necessitates acknowledgment of the inviolability
of "the Person"--acknowledgment of the status of the other
as one who ought always to be respected. This is as close
as Vivas comes to an "absolutistic" ethic, since he insists upon the difficulties we human beings have in
determining the relative worth of the values that comprise
a part of our world and which "require" our recognition
and espousal.

Vivas first suggests here his distinction between creation and discovery, so important in his aesthetics, in
his insistence that the "resolution of a radical moral
perplexity" often brings about a transformation of the
moral personality--as determined by those values we es-
pouse--through the discovery of other values that require
our recognition and espousal. Also provides a lengthy
criticism of the naturalistic theory of the origins of
conscience, or the "Super-Ego," an avenue of approach to
his philosophy of culture--his argument against reductionism, or the view that the only way to study man is
the way we study physical objects.

A1a   *The Moral Life and the Ethical Life.* Chicago: Henry
      Regnery Co., Gateway Press, 1963. xxviii + 292 pp.

      A paperback reprint of Parts II and III of the
      above book with a section entitled "In Lieu of Part
      One" written by Vivas to replace Part I of the
      original book.

A2 *Creation and Discovery: Essays in Criticism and Aesthetics.*
    New York: Noonday Press, Inc., 1955. xiv + 306 pp.

    1. Literary Criticism: "Dreiser, an Inconsistent
Mechanist" (C22), "Henry and William" (C43), "Kafka's
Distorted Mask" (C51), "The Two Dimensions of Reality in
The Brothers Karamazov" (C61); 2. Problems of Aesthetics:
"What Is a Poem?" (C71), "A Definition of the Aesthetic
Experience" (C20), "Literature and Knowledge" (C64), "The
Object of the Poem" (C67), "Naturalism and Creativity"
(C54a); 3. Theory of Criticism: "Criticism, Intrinsic and
Extrinsic" (C74), "The Objective Correlative of T.S.
Eliot" (C46), "The Objective Basis of Criticism" (C53);
4. Aesthetic Theories: "Four Notes on I.A. Richards'
Aesthetic Theory" (C15), "A Note on the Emotion in Dewey's
Theory of Art" (C25), "Jordan's Defense of Poetry" (C70),

"Aesthetics and the Theory of Signs" (C75), "Allen Tate as Man of Letters" (C69).

Brings together some of Vivas' most important essays in aesthetics and criticism. Of special interest is "The Object of the Poem," a rather technical but significant explanation of how the poem is *both* a work of art, and as such phenomenal, *and* a creative discovery of values that subsist independent of the poem and are found "in and through the language of the poem." The essay also notes that through his discovery of values the poet becomes "creator of culture," since once his audience becomes familiar with the poet's work "the values are isolated from the poem and espoused, and the meanings are institutionalized and thus given actuality in men's actions." All of these essays reflect Vivas' concerns with such themes as the creative discovery of the artist/poet--*contra* naturalism which likens creation to "problem solving"; the world as we come to know it is constituted by the categories we first find imagistically in works of art, in the form of values and meanings that we intuit faster than thought and which cannot therefore be considered "knowledge," since life imitates art rather than the other way 'round; literature is primarily art and the function of the critic is to enable spectators to deepen and enrich their aesthetic experience while gaining an understanding of the work itself. Throughout, Vivas stresses the objectivity of values, the legitimacy of criticism, and the need to focus attention on the work under examination.

A2a   *Creation and Discovery: Essays in Criticism and Aesthetics.* Chicago: Henry Regnery Co., 1966.

    A paperback version of A2. Complete and unaltered.

A2b   *Creation and Discovery: Essays in Criticism and Aesthetics.* Toronto: Longmans Green and Co., 1955. 460 pp.

    The Canadian edition of A2. Complete and unaltered.

A2c   *Creazione e Scoperta, Saggi di critica e di estetica.* Bologna: Il Mulino, 1958. xiii + 351 pp.

    An Italian translation of A2.

A3 *D.H. Lawrence: The Failure and Triumph of Art.* Evanston: Northwestern University Press, 1960. xvi + 302 pp.

Introductory: The Two Lawrences (C78). The Failure of Art: Ch. I, *Aaron's Rod*; Ch. II, *Kangaroo*; Ch. III, *The*

Plumed Serpent I; Ch. IV, *The Plumed Serpent* II; Ch. V,
Lady Chatterley's Lover; Ch. VI, Lawrence Imitates Law-
rence. The Triumph of Art: Ch. VII, *Sons and Lovers*; Ch.
VIII, *The Rainbow*; Ch. IX, The Form of *Women in Love*; Ch.
X, The Substance of *Women in Love* (C79). Appendix--The
Constitutive Symbol.

A book-length critical study, which demonstrates the
application of Vivas' aesthetics to his criticism (on this
point, see F1). Lawrence's major books are evaluated in
light of Vivas' contention that the works of a poet succeed
or fail *as art* to the extent to which they do or do not
contain "a powerful aesthetic organization of values and
disvalues, the matter of experience as grasped by a gifted
mind and transmuted and informed by it." The successful
result is an object of art capable of holding the spectator's "intransitive attention by embodying immanent meanings [and values]." The artist "exhibits dramatically,"
and does not imitate or provide "truth." Rather, "a poet
has another job to do than preach the dreary lessons
Lawrence tries to preach [in his lesser works]. The poet's
job is important because no one else can do it for him,
while the preaching can be done by others who are usually
better qualified to do it than are poets."
Examples of "pure poetry" among Lawrence's major works
are *The Rainbow*, *Women in Love*, and, to a lesser extent,
Sons and Lovers. The rest suffer because the poet fails
to "inform the matter of his experience" successfully and
the values of the man "have spilled over into the art
without having been subjected to the process of informing
and transubstancing and the result is that the work is
turbid."
Contains an important Appendix entitled "The Constitutive
Symbol," which invites comparison between Vivas' analysis
and Jung's notion of "Archetypes" (see Vivas' "On Aesthetics
and Jung," C125), because they are "beyond discursive
language" and do not yield an "exact conceptual statement
of their meaning." These symbols are found in the language
of the poem and suggest meanings and values through their
symbolic presentation. An example in Lawrence's novella
St. Mawr is St. Mawr himself, who "is what he is, he does
not *represent* anything abstract, whether deep forces of
life or shallow ones, nor does he *stand* for anything. He
embodies, incarnates, renders, *is* vitality and potency.
That is why he is a genuine symbol.... The expression
'deep forces of life' represents what St. Mawr *is*...."
This echoes Vivas' claim that art *qua* art does not imitate at all. As a creative endeavor, it *presents* in
vivid immediacy to the human imagination the substance

of art which upon later reflection can become constitutive
of culture, the symbolic world of man comprised of art,
religion, science, and morality.

A3a   *D.H. Lawrence: The Failure and Triumph of Art.*
        Bloomington: Indiana University Press, 1964.

        A reissue of item A3 in paperback in the "Midland
        Book" series of the Indiana University Press.

A4   *The Artistic Transaction and Essays on Theory of Literature.*
        Columbus: Ohio State University Press, 1963. ix + 267 pp.

   PART ONE: Ch. I, "The Artistic Transaction"; Ch. II,
"Literature and Ideology" (C95); Ch. III, "The Substance of
Tragedy" (C96); Ch. IV, "In Defense of Non-Objective Art"
(C84); Ch. V, "Animadversions on Imitation and Expression"
(C87). PART TWO: Ch. VI, "Contextualism Reconsidered"
(C82); Ch. VII, "A Semantic for Humanists" (C72), Ch. VIII,
"Mr. Wimsatt on the Theory of Literature" (C73), Ch. IX,
"The Neo-Aristotelians of Chicago" (C66).

   Six of the essays are reprinted here as they first
appeared, as noted, while the essay that comprises Chapter
I is a complete revision of "A Natural History of the
Aesthetic Transaction," first published in 1944 (C47), in
light of Vivas' abandonment of naturalism for axiological
realism, and two were written especially for this volume.
Chapter I contains an essay of major importance for understanding Vivas' mature philosophy and shows the influence
on his thinking of Croce, Dewey, and Cassirer—as reflected
in the use of the term "transaction." In borrowing this
term (from Dewey) Vivas says that he wants "to emphasize
that our relationship to art is a 'trans-action' ... in
which each term affects the other." The essay is an
exercise in the phenomenology of art, whereby Vivas strives
to describe the distinctively *aesthetic*, and differentiate
it from other modes of human awareness.
   Vivas also stresses the difference between the "residential" and the "non-residential" aspects of art, a distinction borrowed from DeWitt Parker, and the need to meet art
on its own terms rather than to go through it to something
else or to read extraneous meanings into it. Once again,
Vivas stresses that art does not provide "knowledge" in the
strict sense of this term, though it does provide the
elements out of which knowledge and, indeed, the world as
object-of-knowledge is constituted.
   The second part of the book contains several essays and
review articles that defend "contextualist" criticism

against a variety of objections and emphasize the differences
between this type of criticism, which is fundamentally
formalistic, and the criticism of such writers as Philip
Wheelwright, W.K. Wimsatt, R.S. Crane, W.R. Keast, Richard
McKeon, Norman Maclean, Elder Olson, and Bernard Weinberg.

A5   *Contra Marcuse*. New Rochelle, N.Y.: Arlington House,
       1971. 236 pp.

Contains a preface and twenty-four chapters, untitled,
which comprise a self-styled "polemical" essay "directed
at [Herbert] Marcuse's savage indictment of our society,"
and marks Vivas' growing concern with social problems and
the preservation of human values.

Not an "academic" book in the narrow sense of this term,
by Vivas' own admission, it does contain some arresting
and thought-provoking philosophical arguments. Of greatest
interest in this regard is Vivas' argument in Chapters 15
and 16 directed against Marcuse's hedonism, or the view
that goodness is equivalent to pleasure. Vivas distinguishes
between "needs" and "desires" and argues that "need" is a
normative concept having reference to what man *ought* to
want in contrast with what he *does* want, in fact. Determination of "vital needs" must be made in a thoroughly empirical
manner in light of man's highest potentiality. In this regard, not only does man need to keep his body alive, he
needs beauty to keep his spirit alive as well. In the end
it is Vivas' concern with the human spirit and the values
that comprise human personalities and human possibilities
that forces a break with the shallow hedonism and the
"dystopian" theories of Marcuse.

It is important to note that Vivas' conservatism, and
his attack against Marcuse, are born of his axiological
realism and his claim, arising from his reading of "unmitigated" tragedies, that evil is ineluctable; the cult
of progress is a delusion and would destroy the good along
with the bad.

This book undoubtedly signals the emergence of Vivas as
a major intellectual conservative pitted against an "aprioristic" progressive liberalism that would, as Dostoevsky
and Nietzsche saw in the nineteenth century, destroy man's
freedom and spirit in the trade for bread and miracles.

A5a   *Contra Marcuse*. New York: Dell Publishing Co.,
        1972. 236 pp.

Paperback reprint of A5.

A6   *Two Roads to Ignorance: A Quasi Biography.*   Carbondale and
      Edwardsville: The University of Southern Illinois Press,
      1979.   xiii + 304 pp.

      Preface; Acknowledgments; Ch. I, The Mixed-Up Twenties;
Ch. II, More Confusions; Ch. III, State at Midland City;
Ch. IV, Teachers and "Teachers" (C126); Ch. V, Alonzo as
"Teacher" (C127); Ch. VI, Borrowed Thoughts; Ch. VII, The
Red Thirties; Ch. VIII, Objections to Marx; Ch. IX, The
Blind Spots of Naturalism; Ch. X, Pragmatism and the Tragic
Sense of Life (C133); Ch. XI, Naturalism's Theory of Value;
Ch. XII, The Question of Origins; Ch. XIII, From Protohominid
to Homo Sapiens; Ch. XIV, Darwinians on Human Culture; Ch.
XV, On Human Origins: Freud and Others (C130); Ch. XVI,
Alonzo Too Was Guilty; Ch. XVII, The Moral Life and the
Ethical Life; Ch. XVIII, Politics or Idiocy?; Ch. XIX, Art
and Knowledge; Ch. XX, Was the Quest a Failure? (C132).

      A unique book that combines a third-person biography--
of Alonzo Quijano--with an explanation of the development
of Vivas' philosophical thought.   Breaks at Chapter IX with
a criticism of naturalism to begin the more formal elements
of the treatise.   Prior to that, Vivas recounts his earlier
years and his various "apprenticeships" in academies of
"higher learning."   A scathing account of intolerance, petti-
ness, back-biting, and politicking in academia set against a
background of social turmoil at a time when Marxism seemed
to many intellectuals to offer answers to impossible questions, and science was the only suitable object of worship.
      The pivotal concept that marks the transition from natu-
ralism and scientism to Vivas' later thought is "tragedy."
The absence of a tragic sensibility among pragmatists, for
example, made Vivas search for a more adequate philosophy
[C38, C50, C54, C81.   Also cf. Sidney Hook's rejoinder,
G21].   "... tragedy is an essential element of the universe
in a sense that a naturalist--who believes that everything
that happens is a part of Nature--would deny ... human
events that constitute [a] tragedy are connected morally
and not merely by means of value free causal connections
with the universe."   On the other hand, "an adequate philosophy, one equal to the requirements of a whole man, not of
a man with a vision dimmed by scientific faith and a
Pelagian optimism, should have something to say about the
cluster of values and disvalues that men cannot successfully
turn their faces from."
      The middle chapters mark some of the best arguments in
Vivas' *oeuvre* against "scientism," or the view that would
seek to provide an exhaustive, value-free account of man on
the model of the exact sciences.   Interestingly, Vivas

argues that this hope for reducing persons to things is a
matter of *faith* on the part of naturalism, since the evidence would suggest that there are unknowables that cannot
be ignored without misrepresentation. These chapters mark
a transition to the final chapters where Vivas reiterates
his concern for the reality of value in a world of fact.
These arguments echo the arguments of Philip Wheelwright
used against Vivas' own early version of naturalism (G43).

B

BOOKS EDITED

B1 *The Problems of Aesthetics: A Book of Readings.* New York:
    Holt, Rinehart and Winston, Inc., 1953. xiii + 639 pp.
    (In collaboration with Murray Krieger).

I. The Discipline of Aesthetics. "The Nature, the Teach-
ing and the Problems of Aesthetics," by the Editors (C65);
"Artists, Critics, and Philosophers," by Louis Arnand Reid;
"Psychology and Art Today: A Summary and Critique," by
Douglas N. Morgan. II. The Nature of Art. "A Definition
of Art," by Jacques Maritain; "Art as Intuition," by Benedetto Croce; "The Nature of Art," by DeWitt Parker; "Science,
Art and Technology," by Charles W. Morris. III. The Creative Act. "The 'Germ' of a Story," by Henry James; "The
Art of Fiction," by Henry James; "Bergson's Theory of Art,"
by T.E. Hulme; "The Creative Process in the Artist's Mind,"
by S. Alexander; "The Relation of the Poet to Day-Dreaming,"
by Sigmund Freud; "Neurotic and Artist," by Sigmund Freud;
"On the Relation of Analytic Psychology to Poetic Art," by
Carl Gustav Jung. IV. The Aesthetic Object. GENERIC
TRAITS. "The Elements of Aesthetic Surface in General,"
by D.W. Prall; "Form," by G.W. Gotschalk; "The Aesthetic
Hypothesis," by Clive Bell; "Perception, Meaning, and the
Subject-Matter of Art," by Arnold Eisenberg; "The Formal
Structure of the Aesthetic Object," by Benbow Richie;
"Iconic Signs and Expressiveness," by Isabel Creed Hunger-
land. VARIOUS ARTS. "The Analysis of the Literary Work
of Art," by René Wellek and Austin Warren; "Notes of a
Painter," by Henri Matisse; "Outlines of Musical Form,"
by W.H. Hadow. V. The Aesthetic Experience. VARIETIES OF
AESTHETIC EXPERIENCE. "Varieties of Aesthetic Experience,"
by Henri Delacroix; "Types of Response to Color," by Albert
R. Chandler; "Types of Listeners," by Albert R. Chandler;
"Varieties of Musical Experience," by Vernon Lee. INTER-
PRETATIONS OF AESTHETIC EXPERIENCE. "The Aesthetic Experi-
ence as Pleasure," by Henry Rutgers Marshall; "Empathy," by
Herbert Sidney Langfield; "Having an Experience," by John
Dewey; "The Expression of Emotion," by R.G. Collingwood;

"The Aesthetic Attitude," by Curt John Ducasse; "The
Aesthetic Feelings," by Curt John Ducasse; "Emotion," by
Stephen C. Pepper; "The Aesthetic Response as Organization
of Attitudes," by I.A. Richards; "Psychical Distance as a
Factor in Art and an Aesthetic Principle," by Edward Bullough;
"A Definition of the Aesthetic Experience," by Eliseo Vivas
(C20). VI. The Aesthetic Judgment. THE FUNCTION OF CRITI-
CISM. "The Three Aspects of Criticism," by T.M. Greene;
"A Burden for Critics," by R.P. Blackmur. THE VALIDITY OF
THE AESTHETIC JUDGMENT. "The Authority of Criticism," by
George Boas; "Relativism Again," by Bernard C. Heyl; "The
Social-Historical Relativity of Aesthetic Value," by Arthur
Child; "The Objectivity of Beauty," by C.E.M. Joad. VII.
The Functions of Art. ART AND RELIGION. "The Religious
Function of Art," by Leo Tolstoy. ART AND SOCIETY. "Poetry
and Society," by Nicolai Bukharin; "Justification of Art,"
by George Santayana; "Art and Happiness," by George Santa-
yana. ART AND MORALITY. "Poetry and Morals: A Relation
Reargued," by W.K. Wimsatt, Jr.; "The Moral Effect of Art,"
by Sidney Zink. ART AS AUTONOMOUS. "Poetry for Poetry's
Sake," by A.C. Bradley; "Art and Ethics," by Clive Bell.
ART AND TRUTH. "Poetry and Beliefs," by I.A. Richards;
"Art, Language, and Truth," by Morris Weitz; "The Cognitive
Content of Art," by Dorothy Walsh; "Aesthetic Knowledge,"
by Philip Leon.

An anthology that reflects Vivas' major concerns in
aesthetics. The opening essay was written by Vivas, in
cooperation with Murray Krieger, and is a general introduction to "the central and heterogeneous problems which
... constitute the discipline of aesthetics" and to this
book in particular. Of special interest is the diagram
employed to show the relationships among the "factors or
components which are required in order that art-objects
be produced and used in human society." This diagram
displays the notion of "interaction" between the spectator
and the object as well as that between the artist and the
object at the time of its creation, and the relation between all three and society. In this last regard, the
diagram is informative in grasping how it is that the
artist is "creator of culture." (See facing page.) In dis-
cussing the art object, Vivas notes the following relationship between the critic and the aesthetician: "Between aesthetics and criticism no separation ought to exist.... The
aesthetician goes or ought to go for his subject matter a-
mong others to the critic; he functions as critic when he
goes for it to the art product directly available to him.
And the critic uses conceptions which are examined and criti-
cised by the aesthetician, but whose utility is tested by

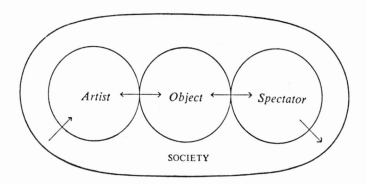

the critic. Custom ... assigns to aesthetics the region of
abstract analysis and theoretical system building, and to
criticism the determination of meanings and values expressed
in the actual objects of art in order to put them in the pos-
session of spectators."

The argument of the introduction is expanded in Vivas'
essay "The Nature of Aesthetics" (C68).

C

ESSAYS AND REVIEW ARTICLES

C1 "Pio Baroja y Nessi." *The Literary Review* (December 23, 1922), p. 339.

Expresses regret over the widespread ignorance of Spanish writers by the American "literate" public, and provides background information about the culture of Pio Baroja y Nessi. Of special concern is the "generation of '98"--a group of men who were profoundly influenced by Spain's defeat at the hands of the U.S. Points to the "universal appeal" of Baroja, "the first Spanish novelist of today."

C2 "Where Conquest Would Be Freedom." *The Independent* 112 (April 26, 1924), pp. 223-5 and 229.

Argues in favor of American imperialism on the grounds that Latin American nations are culturally and economically backward. By conquest "the Yankee" would awaken the "consciousness of the lower classes." If not, he would at least "raise the country's standard of living a hundred-fold." In short, "industrial barbarism and enslavement are preferable to feudal barbarism," and that is the condition of Venezuela and Latin America generally.

C3 "The Unknown Critic." *The Nation* 119 (December 10, 1924), pp. 638-9.

Anonymously characterizes himself as a critic who "is mainly interested in life as expressed in literature." In that role he "finds vicarious self-realization by giving a meaning to the world of the artist." The third-person narrative style suggests the pattern followed in *Two Roads to Ignorance* (A6).

C4 "The Critic's Answer." *The Nation* 123 (December, 1926), pp. 600-1.

Raises the question of whether "conditions in our times in America are such as to allow the birth of great art,"

and responds in the negative, because ours is an age in
flux and artists are a part of that flux. It is thus not
possible to understand it or to "express it fully."

C5   "The Ideal College." *The New Issue* (March, 1927). (Infor-
      mation incomplete.)

      Criticizes by broad use of sarcasm and humor the condi-
tions which Vivas encountered at the University of Wisconsin under the presidency of Glenn Frank.

C6   "Notes." *The New Issue* (March, 1927). (Information in-
      complete.)

      Reflections about three men of note: Havelock Ellis, who
is chided for being too vague and "mystical"; Anatole
France, "a pretty bundle of platitudes"; and Thoreau, for
whom Vivas had the highest regard (see C9).

C7   "Recent Spanish Literature." *The Nation* 124, 3227 (May 11,
      1927), pp. 530-1.

      Provides an overview of recent literature in Spain.
Notes with regret that the "generation of '98"--Benavente,
Baroja, Unamuno--are on the wane; but a small group of
younger men--Valle Inclán, Marquina, Moreno Villa, and
Ramón de Basterra--is on the rise.

C8   "A Note on Modern Tragedy." *Wisconsin Literary Magazine*
      27, 1 (November, 1927), pp. 11-6.

      Traces the growth of "modern tragedy" out of classical
tragedy. The former evidences broader "ethical and psychological forces," but is mere pathos, man pitted against
society rather than the gods. Contrasts a contemporary
view (Dreiser's) with that of Shakespeare.

C9   "Thoreau: The Paradox of Youth." *The New Student* 7, 23
      (March 7, 1928), pp. 5-9.

      Points out precisely how it is that Thoreau was not
"merely an understudy of Emerson." Castigates Thoreau for
being too idealistic, a fault that results in narrowness
of vision and loss of wisdom. "... there is something more
important than the intense idealism of youth and its fiery
vision--and that is the penetration of wisdom. And wisdom
is given only to age: age, not in its quantitative but in
its qualitative sense. And this Thoreau, though he lived
long enough to acquire it, never did acquire. He died
a youth."

C10 "Culture's Feet of Clay." *The New Student* 8, 1 (October, 1928), pp. 6-8.

Defends the materialistic (economic) interpretation of history and culture, and applies this to an understanding of the *raison d'être* of the modern college. Argues that colleges are the "factories wherein the metaphysics of the system are manufactured."

C11 "Robinson Jeffers." *The New Student* 8, 7 (April, 1929), pp. 13-5.

Celebrates the "largeness" of Jeffers whose greatness is limited by his misanthropy "in the full swing of hatred.... He hates man and men and the blade of his hatred truncates his greatness." At the same time, it can be said of Jeffers that his language never "obtrudes upon the burden of meaning"; in his poetry "the course of events sweep us on because they are conveyed in a language which only rarely, and that almost always in his shorter poems, makes itself felt to the reader." This view anticipates Vivas' later contextualist view of poetry, and marks Vivas as one of the first critics to note that Jeffers' misanthropy flaws his poetry.

C12 "Paginas de un diario." *Elite* (Caracas, Venezuela), Año VI, 266 (October 18, 1930), pp. 15-6.

Eight pages from Vivas' diary, translated into Spanish, containing reflections "sketched at random into words" on books, people, and art.

C13 "Wisconsin's Experimental College." *The Nation* 132, 3429 (March 25, 1931) pp. 322-5.

Describes and analyzes Alexander Meikeljohn's experimental college at the University of Wisconsin. Questions whether the college achieved its objectives. Specifically, it charges that the experiment divorces learning and wisdom. (Cf. Meikeljohn's response, G29.)

C14 "Education and the Crisis." *The New Student* (May, 1934), pp. 9 and 13.

Responds to Sam Sillen's claim, in the same issue, that University professors are in danger of losing contact with "the larger world," by defending knowledge for its own sake.

C15   "Four Notes on I.A. Richards' Aesthetic Theory." *The*
        Philosophical Review 44, 4 (July, 1935), pp. 354-67.

        Criticizes Richards' reduction of value to individual
        "satisfaction" by showing that Richards does not derive
        his view from science (psychology) but has "injected it
        from without." The seeds are planted for Vivas' later
        critique of naturalism.

        C15a "Four Notes on I.A. Richards' Aesthetic Theory."
                Creation and Discovery (A2), pp. 209-21.

                Reprint of C15.

C16   "Art, Morals, and Propaganda." *International Journal of*
        Ethics 46, 1 (October, 1935), pp. 82-95.

        Counters the view, widely held at the time, that art
        must seek social melioration or it is useless. Suggests
        the "autotelic" nature of art so central in contextualism,
        and introduces the notion of the "intrinsic" or "resident"
        value of a poem. For the first time in print, Vivas
        suggests another theme that becomes central to his theory
        later on: "Art affects life because it teaches us how to
        see, how to hear, how to feel; because it creates for us
        'norms of feeling,' and 'categories of perception' which
        mold unconsciously our subsequent experience in subtle
        and diverse ways."

C17   "The Aesthetic Judgment." *The Journal of Philosophy* 33,
        3 (January 30, 1936), pp. 57-69.

        Basing the discussion implicitly on the same assumptions
        later to be expounded in "A Note on Value" (C18), Vivas
        seeks to save the aesthetic judgment from subjectivity by
        arguing that aesthetic judgments can claim objectivity in
        the sense that the judgment refers to qualities in or on
        the object. These qualities constitute the values that,
        as tertiary qualities, are parasitic on the secondary
        qualities of objects. The normative authority of the
        judgment is grounded on objective qualities the presence
        or absence of which in an object can be discussed.

C18   "A Note on Value." *The Journal of Philosophy* 33, 21
        (October 8, 1936), pp. 568-75.

        Develops Vivas' attack on naturalism by examining the
        Hobbesian view that value is constituted by desire.
        Argues that values are objective either for the individual
        or the group to which he belongs because they are ruled by
        an implicit or explicit rule that can be discovered and
        are hence open to criticism and correction.

C19 "A Note on the Question of 'Class Science.'" *Marxist Quarterly* 1, 3 (October-December, 1937), pp. 437-46.

Employs the same argument against the presumed autonomy of science that some critics later used against Vivas' view that art is "autotelic." Science, insists Vivas, "enjoys a high degree of autonomy," but "it is never altogether complete, since scientists, compartmentalized though they may be, do not really live in isolation from their culture, and their mental processes and the very conceptions which they use in their work cannot be insulated from their daily, ordinary, non-professional experience." [See Sutton, on the "referential" nature of the poet's language: "The Contextualist Dilemma--or Fallacy?" (G38); Sutton, "Contextualist Theory and Criticism as a Social Act," (G39). Also, see C21 and C78 below.]

C20 "A Definition of the Aesthetic Experience." *The Journal of Philosophy* 34, 23 (November 11, 1937), pp. 628-34.

Denies that emotion is a part of the definition of the aesthetic experience and insists instead that the experience be defined in terms of "rapt" attention, or the "intransitive apprehension of the objects' immanent meanings and values in their full presentational immediacy." Also develops Vivas' phenomenalism, his view that the mind is "to some extent constitutive of the manner in which it apprehends" values.

C20a "Sobre la experiencia estetica." *Revista del Caribe* (September, 1941).

Translation of C20 into Spanish.

C20b "A Definition of the Aesthetic Experience." *Creation and Discovery* (A2), pp. 93-9.

Reprint of C20.

C21 "Reality in Art." *University of Kansas City Review* 4, 1 (Autumn, 1937), pp. 437-46.

Distinguishes the aesthetic mode of apprehension from the practical and scientific and in so doing shows why his criticisms of the notion of scientific autonomy (C19) are inappropriate when applied to art. "Neither the practical nor the scientific mind detains itself before objects or events for their own sake. When it does, it undergoes an aesthetic ... experience." Suggests, in the end, his later distinction between the "residential" and

the "non-residential" aspects of art--the one constituted
by the aesthetic experience of art when taken "seriously,"
and the other "offered in retrospect," when one reflects
on the referential meanings found in the language of the
poet.

C22   "Dreiser, an Inconsistent Mechanist." *Ethics* 48, 4
        (July, 1938), pp. 498-508.

Points out the radical contradiction in Dreiser's work
between his borrowed philosophic dogmas and his grasp of
life as evidenced in his novels. According to his
mechanistic philosophy, life is meaningless. But in his
novels his characters suffer success and failure and are
moved towards goals that give their lives meaning, purpose,
significance. The essay has been one of Vivas' most
successful essays in literary criticism if one judges by
the frequency with which it has been referred to--favorably
or adversely.

C22a   "Dreiser, an Inconsistent Mechanist." Kazin, Alfred,
          and Shapiro, Charles, eds., *The Stature of Theodore
          Dreiser: A Critical Survey of the Man and His Work*.
          Bloomington: Indiana University Press, 1955, pp.
          237-45.

          Reprint of C22.

C22b   "Dreiser, an Inconsistent Mechanist." *Creation and
          Discovery* (A2), pp. 3-16.

          Reprint of C22.

C23   "Nature, Common Sense and Science." *Philosophy of Science*
        5, 3 (July, 1938), pp. 300-9.

Defines the "real" as determined by a particular tech-
nique and manner of selection. Defends the objective,
inter-subjective status of the real (*contra* idealism) as
an assumption demanded by "the knowledge activity itself."
Idealism forgets that the "end terms of analysis are not
the exclusive constituents of the things from which we
start," i.e., that the initial selection of ideas deter-
mines the line of inquiry that later equates the ideal with
the real. A most provocative essay, and one that shows
how Vivas would meet the argument of some of his critics
that his own phenomenalism is inconsistent with his realism:
real objects can be regarded as phenomenal objects when
regarded from the perspective of *knowing*; as objects they
are nonetheless real. (See also C20 and cf. Lee Brown's
critique, G6.)

C24   "The Use of Art." *The Journal of Philosophy* 35, 15
       (July 21, 1938), pp. 406-11.

       Argues that the uses art has frequently determine our
       responses to it. "Agnostics and atheists read religious
       poetry at a tremendous discount." Nevertheless, in
       "aesthetic art" (i.e., art that has no use, or moral
       purpose), there are deeper beliefs that comprise its
       value and we can respond to these deeper beliefs whether
       we share the poet's particular beliefs or not. Vivas
       argues elsewhere (*Artistic Transaction*, pp. 57-62) that
       the surface of the poem can make it impossible for us to
       respond to the deeper values that comprise its values as
       art. The implication of both these claims is that the pre-
       sumably relative status of the value that poetry has re-
       flects the conditions under which it is apprehended, and
       not the real value of the poetry itself (see G3 and G19).

C25   "A Note on the Emotion in Mr. Dewey's Theory of Art."
       The Philosophical Review 47, 5 (September, 1938), pp.
       527-31.

       Develops the view that art need not arouse emotion and
       cannot therefore be defined in terms of emotion. Emotion
       is self-conscious and the aesthetic experience (as Dewey
       admits) is not. Suggests the view, developed later, that
       feeling is attendant upon the aesthetic experience, as
       are the objective characters in the object, but emotion
       is not. (See C20 and *Artistic Transaction*, p. 193 *et pas-
       sim*.)

       C25a   "A Note on the Emotion in Mr. Dewey's Theory of Art."
               Creation and Discovery (A2), pp. 223-8.

               Reprint of C25.

C26   "Force in Empirical Ethics." *Ethics* 49, 1 (October,
       1938), pp. 85-92.

       Expresses the concern Vivas felt about the fact that
       "empirical" ethics cannot offer a moral resolution to
       moral perplexities. This concern developed and led to
       the publication of *The Moral Life and the Ethical Life*
       (A1)--especially the criticisms of naturalism found in
       Part I of that work (deleted from the paperback edition).

C27   "The Philosophy of Control." Review of Mead, George
       Herbert, *The Philosophy of the Act*. *Partisan Review*
       6, 1 (Fall, 1938), pp. 113-7.

       Expresses Vivas' approval of those aspects (especially)
       of Mead's work that influenced Vivas' own thinking,

notably his epistemology as seen in C20 and C23. In
passing, Vivas notes the "urgent" need of our day "to
replace the current subjectivistic theories with a theory
which does justice to the essentially social and objective
nature of value."

C28   "The Fanatic as Type." *The Sewanee Review* 47, 2 (April,
         1939), pp. 166-74.

         Attacks the sort of absolutist that Vivas abhors and
whom he carefully dissociates himself from in both *The
Moral and the Ethical Life* (A1) and *Two Roads to Ignorance*
(A7) (pp. 187ff. and 246ff.). Holds the scientist up as
a paragon of open-mindedness in the best Deweyan tradition.

C29   "John Dewey's Achievement." *Partisan Review* 6, 3
         (Spring, 1939), pp. 79-91.

         Sings Dewey's praises in a voice young with enthusiasm.
Stops short of total endorsement only at the threshold to
Dewey's political thought. The essay marks the height of
Vivas' commitment to Dewey's version of naturalism and
is particularly instructive in showing the influence of
Dewey's thinking on Vivas' epistemology--as seen in earlier
essays on science--and aesthetics. In this latter regard
Vivas is particularly taken with Dewey's notion of the
aesthetic object as "emerging" in the aesthetic experience
and with Dewey's description itself, its completeness and
its unity. In the end it is Dewey's naturalistic theory
of value that Vivas will find inadequate, but this essay
suggests that at the time of this writing its adequacy had
not yet been tested and found wanting.

C30   "The New Encyclopedists." *The Kenyon Review* 1, 2 (Spring,
         1939), pp. 159-68.

         Defends the unity of science movement with which Vivas
was in sympathy at the time. Contains an interesting
summary of C.W. Morris' theory of meaning and evidences
a strong pro-scientistic and anti-metaphysical bias
that is remarkable in light of Vivas' later views. (See
also C75.)

C31   "Finalidad del arte." *Revista Nacional de Cultura*
         (Caracas, Venezuela) 8 (June, 1939), pp. 3-5.

         Translation in abbreviated form of "The Use of Art,"
C24.

C32 "Value and Fact." *The Philosophy of Science* 6, 4
         (October, 1939), pp. 432-45.

   Argues for a scientific treatment of "the phenomena of
values." Defends "objective relativism" against subjec-
tivism and "the type of objectivism which detaches value
from human interest." Vivas will later argue against
this view that we desire valuable objects because they
are desirable, that they contain qualities that exhibit
"requiredness" (C45). Values are not ours; we are theirs.

C33 "The Legacy of Freud." *The Kenyon Review* 2, 2 (Spring,
         1940), pp. 173-85.

   Insists that the scientific value of Freud's doctrines
is low, while, at the same time, the philosophical value
is considerable. Anticipates a later view (A1) when he
notes that Freud's account of "conscience" is inadequate,
but contends that, on balance, "in development of an
adequate concept of man the spirit if not the actual
doctrines of Freud will have to play a central rôle."

C34 "Ethical Empiricism and Moral Heteronomy." *The Philo-
         sophical Review* 49, 4 (July, 1940), pp. 447-53.

   Develops the view proposed in "Force in Empirical
Ethics" (C26) that empiricism in moral philosophy leads
to relativism, which leads to heteronomy and the denial
that there is any means other than force to resolve
moral perplexities and settle conflicts. Ethical empiri-
cists are thus believers in "might makes right," a view
accepted by E.B. McGilvary and Charner Perry but rejected
by F.C. Sharp and W.T. Stace. .

C35 "From *The Life of Reason* to *The Last Puritan*." Schilpp,
         Paul, ed., *The Philosophy of George Santayana*. Evanston:
         Northwestern University Press, 1940, pp. 315-50.

   Notes the inconsistency between Santayana's epiphenomenalism and his faith in Reason. Elaborates by pointing out
that epiphenomenalism is at odds with common experience
which regards thought as efficacious. Shows the effects
of this confusion on Santayana's epistemology and his
need to separate "literary" from "scientific" psychology.
Raises a number of probing questions about Santayana's
notion of "harmony" which is a vague notion, disguises a
crypto-relativism, and makes Santayana's attack on barbarism suspect.
   The discussion ends with a short critical study of *The
Last Puritan* and its relation to Santayana's systematic

philosophy. Vivas argues that his poetry reveals the
"utter moral bankruptcy and louring despair" of Santayana's naturalistic philosophy. (See Santayana's reply,
G33.)

C36   "Humanism: A Backward Glance." *T'ien Hsia* 11, 4
         (February, 1941), pp. 301-13.

        Examines critically the retrograde tendencies of the
"Humanism" of Irving Babbitt, an erudite man of little
philosophical training with a contempt for the social
sciences. Comments on the tendency of the Humanists to
regard contemporary events through the thick lenses of a
romantic notion of the past coupled with a "Devil's
theory of history" that singles out Rousseau as "the sole
source of all the pollution of modern life."
        Expresses Vivas' faith (at the time) in science as
"the only means within the reach of men that will enable
them to arrive at whatever truths they will ever possess,"
and defends the naturalistic explanation of "the phenomena
of moral life." Concludes that Babbitt's philosophy "and
with it that of the Humanists who follow him is no philosophy at all but a nest of confusions."

C37   "Lawrence's Problems." *The Kenyon Review* 3, 1 (Winter,
         1941), pp. 83-94.

        Seeks to focus critical attention away from the problem
of Lawrence the man to what Lawrence *says*. Vivas argues
that "the central burden of Lawrence's message" is to
separate life from knowledge and stress the former over
the latter: "The end of life *should be* the ecstasy of
intense living," an end rejected by contemporary Western
culture.

C38   "The New Naturalism." *The Kenyon Review* 3, 4 (Autumn,
         1941), pp. 446-59.

        Describes naturalistic views much under discussion at
the time of the essay. Its main interest lies in the
final section wherein Vivas presents several criticisms,
in a mild and diffident manner, of naturalistic philosophy. Of major concern is naturalism's disregard of a
basic mode of human experience--religion--and of fundamental values such as heroism and the tragic sense of life.
This criticism is the first expression in print of a
nascent repudiation of the naturalism Vivas had defended
until this time.

C39 "Language in Action." *American Sociological Review* 4, 1
(Winter, 1942), pp. 91-8.

Presents an unsparing criticism of the "vicious" simpli-
fications to be found in the "science" of semantics--the
popular version of the serious discipline of semiotics.
Semantics, as presented in the two books under review
(*Language in Action* by S.I. Hayakawa and *Language Habits
in Human Affairs* by Irving C. Lee), is held to be a shallow
doctrine accepting uncritically a radical nominalism: its
main concern is to put forth liberal, political, and
social propaganda under the guise of a new science.

C40 "A Communication: Reply to Mr. Wheelwright." *The Kenyon
Review* 4, 1 (Winter, 1942), pp. 91-8.

Defends his views as maintained in "The New Naturalism"
(C38) against several criticisms leveled against them by
Philip Wheelwright in his article "The Failure of Natural-
ism (A Reply to Eliseo Vivas)" (G43).

C41 "On Symbolism." Review of Langer, Suzanne K., *Philosophy
in a New Key*. *The Kenyon Review* 5, 2 (Spring, 1943),
pp. 301-4.

Looks favorably on Langer's book and focuses on her
theory of mind as it differs from the pragmatist's instru-
mental view of the mind. Evidences Vivas' dissatisfaction
with naturalistic theories of mind and his movement toward
the phenomenalistic view that mind is constitutive of the
world.

C42 "Aesthetics as Libertarian Faith." Review of Kallen,
Horace M., *Art and Freedom*. *The Nation* 156, 23 (June
5, 1943), pp. 814-5.

Evidences dissatisfaction with Kallen's naturalism and
nominalism as an inadequate account of the value of art
and its profound effect on culture.

C42a Review of Kallen, Horace M., *Art and Freedom*. *The
Journal of Philosophy* 40, 19 (September, 1943),
pp. 517-23.

Expands some of the seminal ideas suggested by
the earlier review (C42).

C43 "Henry and William (Two Notes)." *The Kenyon Review* 5, 4
(Autumn, 1943), pp. 580-94.

Argues that in their "moral conceptions" William and
Henry James differ widely, but there is an important

resemblance between them "in the way they conceive the
mind's mode of apprehension." Contains an excellent
description of ethical neutrality--a necessary condition
for all art in Vivas' view: "it consists solely in sub-
missiveness to the inner thrust of the dramatic incident
which has been selected for treatment, in humility before
the object's inward dialectic, as against the arrogant
and pre-intended dominance with which the partisan violates,
for his own subjective ends, the autonomy of his material."

C43a   "Henry y William [James]." *Asomante*, Año II, 2, 3
       (September, 1946), pp. 44-55. Reprinted in *A
       Book of Readings*. New York: Crowell, 1971, pp. 3-14.

       Translation into Spanish of C43.

C44 "Art and Life." Shipley, Joseph T., ed., *Dictionary of
     World Literature*. New York: Philosophical Library,
     1943, pp. 49-50.

     Presents for the first time a carefully drawn distinction
     between the "residential" and the "non-residential" value
     of art. "The aesthetic object shocks our attention and
     holds it," and this is what makes the object distinctively
     aesthetic. Hints at Vivas' later view that the artist is
     "creator of culture" by focusing on the distinctive role
     of the artist as informing society's attitudes and im-
     pulses. The non-residential value of art is, however,
     derivative; art's primary value is residential.

C45 "Value." Shipley, Joseph T., ed., *Dictionary of World
     Literature*. New York: Philosophical Library, 1943,
     pp. 607-9.

     Argues the need for value theory to shore up criticism
     if the latter is not to be merely "pragmatic." Defends
     the objectivity of value, its actual presence in objects.
     It is because values are objective that they generate
     interest: value cannot be reduced to interest, simply.

C45a   "Value and Criticism." Shipley, Joseph T., ed.,
       Dictionary of World Literature. Totowa, N.J.:
       Littlefield, Adams and Co., 1966, pp. 435-7.

       Reprint of C45.

C46 "The Objective Correlative of T.S. Eliot." *American
     Bookman* 1, 1 (Winter, 1944), pp. 7-18.

     Exposes the confusion in Eliot's notion that art is an
     objective correlative of emotion and, generally, the view

that art is in any sense of the word mere imitation. It should be noted that years later Eliot himself abandoned this view. (See also C87.)

C46a "The Objective Correlative of T.S. Eliot." Stallman, R.W., ed., *Critiques and Essays in Criticism, 1920-1948*. New York: Ronald Press, 1949.

Reprint of C46.

C46b "The Objective Correlative of T.S. Eliot." *Creation and Discovery*, A2, pp. 161-74.

Reprint of C46.

C47 "A Natural History of the Aesthetic Transaction." Kirkorian, Yervant H., ed., *Naturalism and the Human Spirit*. New York: Columbia University Press, 1944, pp. 96-120.

Expands the view maintained in "A Definition of the Aesthetic Experience" (C20) and marks Vivas as a central figure in naturalism's inner circle--at a time when he was beginning to have doubts about the adequacy of naturalism as a way of understanding human experience.

C48 "The Spanish Heritage." *American Sociological Review* 10, 2 (April, 1945), pp. 184-91.

Reflects Vivas' deep and abiding interest in Latin American history and culture, the character of the people and the values they espoused. Suggests Vivas' concerns with heroism and tragedy once again--a concern that leads to his break with naturalism.

C48a "The Spanish Heritage." Moreno, Francisco José, and Mitrani, Barbara, eds., *Conflict and Violence in Latin American Politics: A Book of Readings*. New York: Crowell, 1971, pp. 3-14.

Reprint of C48.

C49 "Animadversions on Naturalistic Ethics." *Ethics* 56, 3 (April, 1946), pp. 157-77.

Marks the final break with naturalistic ethics and with naturalism in general. Offers a concentrated attack on same in light of several concerns expressed earlier and several not previously mentioned. Clearly a pivotal essay and one that lays the groundwork for the first part of *The Moral Life and the Ethical Life* (A1) and for the "ontic hypothesis" developed in Part II of that work.

C50   "Don Alonzo to the Road Again." Review of Dewey, John,
      Problems of Men, and Hook, Sidney, *Education for Modern
      Man.* *The Western Review* 11, 2 (Winter, 1947), pp. 59-71.

      Contains a sustained attack on Sidney Hook's philosophy
      of education, though it is generally favorable toward
      Dewey. In capsule form we find Vivas' fundamental quarrel
      with naturalism: "Sustaining his positive ends you will
      find in the instrumentalist [in particular] an optimism
      impenetrable by experience and, by implication, of terror
      and pain and a systematic mutilation of the deeper insights
      into those aspects of existence that give birth to the
      Karamazovs, to Gulliver, to Macbeth, or Lear, to the
      visions of Goya and the Oedipus sequence." Of major con-
      cern is the "scientifism" entailed by instrumentalism, the
      conviction that the scientific method is self-sufficient.
      This is idolatry of the worst sort and needs to be tempered
      by "an absorbing interest in human perplexities and baffle-
      ments." The careful reader will also note an increased
      verve and self-confidence in Vivas' style in this essay;
      his biting and acerbic tone is apparent throughout.

C51   "Kafka's Distorted Mask." *The Kenyon Review* 10, 1
      (Winter, 1948), pp. 51-69.

      Stresses Vivas' view that art does not imitate; it
      creates and informs. Contests with "psychoanalytic
      criticism" and "extrinsic criticism" generally and stresses
      the contextualist view. Boldly states the credo of the
      new critics in the following terms: "His [the author's]
      meaning is something not to be better stated abstractly
      in terms of ideas and concepts to be found beyond the
      fable, but within it, at the dramatic level, in the inter-
      relationships thus revealed to exist among the characters
      and between them and the universe.... The picture of the
      world as it presented itself to Kafka was a mythopoetical
      one and it is our business as readers to discover ... its
      own intrinsic meaning.... The labor of criticism ... be-
      gins [with the novel] and what it has to accomplish is a
      reading of Kafka." The remainder of the essay applies
      this principle to *The Castle* and *The Trial*, primarily,
      and to Kafka's work generally.

      C51a "Kafka's Distorted Mask." Ransom, J.C., ed., *The
            Kenyon Critics. Studies in Modern Literature
            from the Kenyon Review.* Cleveland: World Publish-
            ing Co., 1951, pp. 58-74.

            Reprint of C51.

C51b "Kafka's Distorted Mask." Gray, Ronald, ed.,
Kafka: A Collection of Critical Essays. Engle-
wood Cliffs, N.J.: Prentice-Hall, 1962, pp. 133-46.

Reprint of C51.

C51c "Kafka's Distorted Mask." *Creation and Discovery*
(A2), pp. 29-46.

Reprint of C51.

C52 "Julian Huxley's Evolutionary Ethics." *Ethics* 58, 4
(Summer, 1948), pp. 275-84.

Provides for the first time a careful analysis of the
naturalistic account of the "emergence" of conscience.
One can only account for the normative dimension of conscience by viewing it as a response to value (see also
A1). "Guilt," says Vivas, "does not appear when a value-
free force is suppressed by another value-free force but
when a wrong force comes into conflict with a right one....
The sense of moral obligation involves a relationship to
values ... objective to us."

C53 "The Objective Basis of Criticism." *The Western Review*
12, 4 (July, 1948), pp. 197-219.

Stresses the need for theory in criticism and makes a
case for the objectivity of values to which criticism
must refer to avoid cryptosubjectivism. The objectivity
of values makes aesthetic judgments corrigible; it does
not guarantee their correctness. As Vivas notes, "What
objectivity requires, besides the objectivity of the
value, is not that we have consensus, but that we have on
hand means of checking the validity of our judgments.
Infallibility is not possible, but it is not necessary
either."

C53a "The Objective Basis of Criticism." *Creation and
Discovery*, A2, pp. 191-206.

Reprint of C53.

C54 "Two Notes on the New Naturalism." *The Sewanee Review*
56, 3 (July, 1948), pp. 477-509.

Removes all doubt about Vivas' total rejection of
naturalism because of its inability to "do full justice
to the higher religion, morality, and art"--despite the
claims of its proponents to the contrary. The essay also
demonstrates Vivas' forte as a polemicist, and makes the

point Vivas will repeat in his critique of naturalism:
"The new naturalism is as aprioristic in its advocacy of
scientific method as any metaphysician ever was." Of the
naturalistic theory of mind, Vivas charges that there is
lacking any account of human creativity, private experience, or other "submerged processes of the psyche, the
intentional mental direction, the purposive thrust of
the mind, the mind's ability to follow the lead of something which is not pushing it from behind so to speak,
since it is not yet there." Overall, the naturalistic
rejection of what it cannot deal with on its own terms
is the basis for Vivas' rejection of naturalism. The
essay contains for the first time in print Vivas' claim
that the artistic creation is also a discovery, in that
his creation is "as strange and fascinatingly new and unexpected to the artist when he finally brings it forth as
it is to a competent audience."

C54a   "Naturalism and Creativity." Tomas, Vincent, ed.,
          Creativity in the Arts. Englewood Cliffs, N.J.:
          Prentice-Hall, 1964, pp. 84-96.

          A somewhat revised version of the second of "Two
          Notes on the New Naturalism" (C54).

C54b   "Naturalism and Creativity." *Creation and Discovery*
          (A2), pp. 145-60.

          Reprint of C54a.

C55   "Theorists Without Theory." Review of Wellek, René,
          and Warren, Austin, *Theory of Literature*. *The Kenyon
          Review* 12, 1 (Winter, 1949), pp. 161-5.

          Argues that critics need not only a "theory of criticism"
          (as per Wellek and Warren) but "a controlling aesthetic"
          as well. Such an aesthetic need not be explicit, but it
          needs to control theory in such a way as to rule out
          mutually incompatible assumptions and provide a coherent
          and defensible foundation for criticism. (See also C76.)

C56   "The Heresy of Paraphrase." Review of Bowra, C.M., *The
          Creative Experiment*. *Poetry* 75, 4 (January, 1950),
          pp. 217-24.

          Regrets that Bowra's otherwise excellent book "does not
          make clear how [for example] Eliot's dissatisfaction,
          which at one time results in prose works of a scientific
          or of a rhetorical nature ... is also capable of producing
          a poem." Bowra is overly concerned about the function and

and subject matter rather than the informed substance of poetry and enters the critical lists with light theoretical weaponry.

C57 "The Moral Philosophy of Corporate Man." Review of Jordan, E., *The Good Life*. *Ethics* 60, 3 (April, 1950), pp. 188-97.

Generally high in praise of Jordan's book, though it notes that Jordan has not solved "one of the most pressing problems of moral philosophy, to wit, how to resolve moral conflicts morally," and has not provided a fully developed analysis of the concept of "persons." These are problems Vivas set himself in writing *The Moral Life and the Ethical Life* (A1).

C58 "Philosophy for Nineteen Eighty-Four." Review of Sellars, R., et al., *Philosophy for the Future*. *The Sewanee Review* 58, 3 (Summer, 1950), pp. 505-13.

Criticizes at length the twenty-two papers that here present the view of modern materialism and provides an opportunity for Vivas to develop further his objections to naturalistic philosophy, of which materialism is a part.

C59 "The Function of Criticism Today." Harris, Julian, ed., *The Humanities: An Appraisal*. Madison: University of Wisconsin Press, 1950, pp. 49-66.

Presents, among other things, an apology for new criticism as a form of criticism made necessary by the demand for "new receptive capacities" in the face of such post-war literature as *Ulysses* and *The Waste Land*. Additionally, there had occurred a "degradation" in culture creating a gap between the artist and his audience that increased the need for critics with an "intense interest in literature as literature." At the close of the essay Vivas expresses regret that few of the new critics possess a "comprehensive knowledge of the problems of aesthetics."

C59a "The Function of Criticism Today." Harris, Julian, ed., *The Humanities: An Appraisal*. Madison: University of Wisconsin Press, 1962, pp. 49-66.

Second edition of C59.

C60 "The Function of Art in the Human Economy." Harris, Julian, ed., *The Humanities: An Appraisal*. Madison: University of Wisconsin Press, 1950, pp. 143-51.

A second paper by Vivas as a part of the Symposium on
the Humanities in American Society at the University of
Wisconsin in 1949. (See C59.) The paper criticizes the
imitation and expression theories of art in favor of the
view that the artist's activity is a "creative discovery."

C60a "The Function of Art in the Human Economy." Harris,
       Julian, ed., *The Humanities: An Appraisal*.
       Madison: University of Wisconsin Press, 1962,
       pp. 143–51.

       Second edition of C60.

C61 "The Two Dimensions of Reality in *The Brothers Karamazov*."
      The Sewanee Review 59, 1 (January, 1951), pp. 23–49.

      Attacks the view that novels present "doctrines" or
      "views" in the sense of "systematic structures of abstract
      thought" in favor of the view that the novel contains "a
      dramatic organization of life." This view will become a
      cornerstone of Vivas' critical theory.
      On the whole, the essay shows Vivas at his best with a
      searching and sympathetic reading of a complicated
      "poem" laid bare in a clear and compelling prose that
      holds the reader's attention throughout.

C61a "The Two Dimensions of Reality in *The Brothers
       Karamazov*." *Creation and Discovery* (A2), pp.
       47–70.

       Reprint of C61.

C61b "The Two Dimensions of Reality in *The Brothers
       Karamazov*." Wellek, René, ed., *Dostoevsky: A
       Collection of Critical Essays*. Engelwood Cliffs,
       N.J.: Prentice-Hall, 1962, pp. 71–89.

       Reprint of C61.

C62 "Aesthetics from Above." Review of Feibleman, James K.,
      *Aesthetics: A Study of the Fine Arts in Theory and
      Practice. The Western Review* 15, 3 (Spring, 1951),
      pp. 229–34.

      Argues that Feibleman approaches aesthetics "from
      above," which is to say that he is more concerned with
      the resolution of general philosophical problems than he
      is with art. While accepting Feibleman's "axiological
      realism," Vivas insists that the artist's discovery is
      creative and faults the author for ignoring this paradox--
      a paradox that comprises the central thrust of Vivas'
      own aesthetic.

C63 "Criticism and the Little Mags." *The Western Review* 16,
1 (Fall, 1951), pp. 9-18.

Praises the "little mags" as the last vestige of serious
criticism, and as an invaluable aid in molding new critical minds at a time when it is necessary "to teach a
generation how to read." Defends new criticism as the
most productive line of approach to literature, and links
its rise to the evolution of reviews such as *Western*,
Hudson, *Sewanee*, *Partisan*, *Kenyon*, "and their brethren."

C64 "Literature and Knowledge." *The Sewanee Review* 60, 4
(October, 1952), pp. 561-92.

Denies that knowledge in the sense of "that which can
be tested by positive methods" is to be found in literature, on the grounds that such a supposition presupposes
that the novel imitates life, whereas the opposite is
true. Distinguishes between the subject matter and the
substance of the novel, following A.C. Bradley, and argues
that the latter must be grasped aesthetically and as such
is "prior in the order of logic to all knowledge."

C64a "Literature and Knowledge." *Creation and Discovery*
(A2), pp. 101-27.

Reprint of C64.

C65 Introduction to *The Problems of Aesthetics*. New York:
Holt, Rinehart and Winston, 1953, pp. 1-19.

See B1 and C68.

C66 "The Neo-Aristotelians of Chicago." Review of Crane, R.S.,
ed., *Critics and Criticism, Ancient and Modern*. *The
Sewanee Review* 61 (January, 1953), pp. 136-49.

Takes exception to the resurrection of Aristotle's
notion of art as imitation on the grounds that this denies
the creative aspect of art; objects also to the notion
that pleasure is the end of poetry and decries the
"methodological relativism which [is] the philosophic
basis of the school...."

C66a "The Neo-Aristotelians of Chicago." *The Artistic
Transaction*, pp. 243-59.

Reprint of C66.

C67   "The Object of the Poem." *The Review of Metaphysics* 7,
         1 (September, 1953), pp. 19-35.

Clearly one of the two or three central essays in Vivas'
aesthetics, this essay insists that the "object" of the
poem is to be found "in and through the language of the
poem." As grasped aesthetically, the object comprises
the "substance" of the poem which cannot be reduced to
the "matter" of the poem without leaving a residue. But
we can also consider the object of the poem prior to its
embodiment in the poem viewed as linguistic artifact,
and after that as well. Prior to its presentation in
language the object is "prefigured in culture"; posterior
thereto, after reflection, it becomes "constitutive of
culture."

Thus Vivas distinguishes here, as he has stated expressly
elsewhere ("Reply to Some Criticisms," C109), three realms
of being: (1) Subsistence, where the meanings and values
that the poet discovers lie prior to their discovery;
(2) Insistence, where they lie when the artist informs
them and thus creates a self-sufficient object; and (3)
Existence, into which the values enter after they have
been apprehended aesthetically. In a word, "the poem
reveals insistent meanings and values in and through its
linguistic medium, which are not merely nominal projec-
tions of our desires but are revelations through symbolic
representations of subsistent values and meanings, that
therefore have status in being." The notion that the
poem represents does not commit Vivas to an imitation
theory because from the perspective of existence, the
poem is a genuine novelty, a creation of something entirely new which was, *at best*, only "prefigured in culture."
The object of the poem is, therefore, constituted of
those meanings and values that become actual in the poet's
creative discovery and later come to constitute what we
call "culture."

C67a   "The Object of the Poem." Adams, Hazard, ed.,
          Critical Theory Since Plato. New York: Harcourt
          Brace Jovanovich, 1971, pp. 1069-77.

          Reprint of C67.

C67b   "The Object of the Poem." *Creation and Discovery*
          (A2), pp. 129-44.

          Reprint of C67.

C68 "The Nature of Aesthetics." Wild, John, ed., *The Return to Reason*. Chicago: Henry Regnery Co., 1953, pp. 201-17.

Expands the ideas presented in the Introduction to *The Problems of Aesthetics* (C65 and B1).
Contains a long and valuable analysis of the relation between Vivas' conception of aesthetics and the need to embrace axiological realism. Faults the analytic approach to aesthetics because it can only yield "linguistic clarity about confused data," and smacks of theory devoid of practice.

C69 "Allen Tate as a Man of Letters." Review of Tate, Allen, *The Forlorn Demon: Didactic and Critical Essays*. *The Sewanee Review* 62 (Winter, 1954), pp. 131-43.

Defends the man of letters in a positivistic era as one who seeks "a world which will allow us in some measure at least to realize our human destiny." Disagrees with Tate's "historical interpretation" of the birth of the positivistic era with Descartes but is in general agreement that the future will not resemble the past and "the things [we love] are doomed." Of great concern is the death of "the angelic imagination" in the nineteenth century.

C69a "Allen Tate as Man of Letters." Squires, Radcliffe, ed., *Allen Tate and His Work: Critical Evaluations*. Minneapolis: University of Minnesota Press, 1972, pp. 78-91.

Reprint of C69.

C69b "Allen Tate as Man of Letters." *Creation and Discovery* (A2), pp. 267-81.

Reprint of C69.

C70 "Jordan's Defense of Poetry." Review of Jordan, E., *Essays in Criticism*. *Review of Metaphysics* 8, 1 (September, 1954), pp. 162-75.

Praises Jordan's book highly and demonstrates the impact of Jordan and other post-Kantian philosophers--chiefly Croce and Cassirer--on his own thinking. This essay, taken with the one immediately preceding, clearly indicates that Vivas is entering what might be called the "idealist phase" of his thinking. Elements of idealism were present before, but they will hereafter predominate in his thinking about art. The view that Vivas shares

with Jordan, namely, that the role of the artist is
"creator of culture," gets its impetus from this phase
of thinking. Vivas expresses his appreciation of Jordan's
attempt to "harmonize the idealist principle of the constitutive role of knowledge with objectivity, and to
qualify his realism by the idealist principle." Indeed!
It is Vivas' problem as well: the "paradox" of creation
and discovery.

Contains the interesting suggestion, not found elsewhere, that it is not the poet, necessarily, who "creates
culture," but anyone who uses language poetically rather
than merely as a means of communication. The first use
is "constitutive." The second is practical.

C70a "Jordan's Defense of Poetry." *Creation and Dis-*
        covery (A2), pp. 229-47.

        Reprint of C70.

C71 "What Is a Poem?" *The Sewanee Review* 62, 4 (Autumn, 1954),
        pp. 578-97.

Argues the idealist, or phenomenalist, thesis that the
poem exists only during the moment of rapt, intransitive
attention, during the artistic transaction. The poem, as
such, "organizes the primary data of experience that can
be exhibited in and through words," and therefore "puts
the world at our disposal." The poem is self-sufficient,
complete, and unified and as such is capable of sustaining
interest and attention to the poem itself. *In* the language of the poem resides that which is untranslatable;
through the language of the poem we find, on reflection,
"an object that can also be referred to by means of a
more or less carefully contrived paraphrase." The two
"moments" must be carefully distinguished as the immanent
meanings and values we find only in the poem itself (M')
make it possible to grasp our world anew (M").

Upon reflection on the values that reside in the poem
itself, we perceive the world differently, we "constitute"
it with the schema and categories supplied by the poet
who can therefore be said to be creator of culture, "the
man who sees the values [of a particular culture] as they
struggle to be born or who sees those that have already
been born into history but which nobody notices. He is
a midwife and uses the forceps of language."

Of central importance to this view is the contention
that art is *sui generis*: it performs a function no other
mode of human response can perform. It does not yield
knowledge, but it makes knowledge possible.

This essay, together with "The Object of the Poem" (C67), comprises the cornerstone of Vivas' aesthetics and helps to show how Vivas' aesthetics is linked to his axiological realism. (See A1.)

C71a "What Is a Poem?" *Creation and Discovery* (A2), pp. 73-92.

Reprint of C71.

C72 "A Semantics for Humanists." Review of Wheelwright, Philip, *The Burning Fountain*. *The Sewanee Review* 63, 2 (April, 1955), pp. 307-17.

Raises some objections to Wheelwright's notion of "depth meaning" in the context of an otherwise favorable review of his book. Wheelwright fails to distinguish between "the expression of emotion in an aesthetic object ... and the arousal of emotion in the reader or listener." Furthermore, Wheelwright's analysis assumes that the object can be seen as comprised of levels of meaning at the time it is grasped aesthetically, whereas such distinctions can be made only after the aesthetic experience. Vivas insists on the distinctive nature of the object of art and its autonomy and irreducibility, and develops his notion that the object of the poem is to be found *in* and *through* the language of the poem. Vivas concludes with an excellent discussion of the "knowledge" that arises from poetry—which knowledge in not subject to confirmation or the laws of thought: it is not knowledge at all, strictly speaking, but something that precedes knowledge and makes it possible.

C72a Review of Wheelwright, Philip, *The Burning Fountain*. *Perspective, U.S.A.* 14, 14 (January, 1956), pp. 167-75.

Reprint of C72.

C72b "A Semantics for Humanists." *The Artistic Transaction* (A4), pp. 203-15.

Reprint of C72.

C73 "Mr. Wimsatt on the Theory of Literature." Review of Wimsatt, W.K., Jr., *The Verbal Icon: Studies in the Meaning of Poetry*. *Comparative Literature*, 7, 4 (Fall, 1955), pp. 344-61.

Discourses at length, critically and insightfully, on Wimsatt's borrowed notion of the "concrete universal,"

and his "eclecticism" generally which lacks systematic
underpinnings. Criticizes Wimsatt's notion of how a
poem takes on meaning by arguing that the poem does not
assert or represent, it *presents*: it is devoid of cognitive meaning (since the poem is *pre*-cognitive); and rejects Wimsatt's notion that the language of poetry is
iconic on the grounds that this makes art mere imitation.

C73a "Mr. Wimsatt on the Theory of Literature." *The
      Artistic Transaction* (A4), pp. 217-42.

      Reprint of C73.

C74 "Criticism, Intrinsic and Extrinsic." *Creation and Dis-
     covery*, A2, pp. 161-74.

     The first appearance in print of the Mahlon Powell
     Lecture given at Indiana University on July 22, 1952 (E3).
     Examines the two presuppositions of new criticism: that
     art is autotelic, and that there is a distinctive *aesthet-
     ic* response to art. Consents to the "intentional fallacy"
     of Wimsatt and Beardsley and notes that the poet himself
     cannot be considered an expert on the topic of his purpose.
     In short, "the poem supplies all that we need to come into
     possession of it."

C75 "Aesthetics and the Theory of Signs." *Creation and Dis-
     covery*, A2, pp. 249-66.

     The first appearance in print of a part of the second
     Mahlon Powell Lecture given at Indiana University on
     July 24, 1952 (E4), the first part of which appeared as
     "The Object of the Poem" (C67).
     Contains a sustained examination of C.W. Morris'
     "semiotic aesthetics" (see C30), and distinguishes care-
     fully between signs and symbols. Charges that the claim
     that art contains signs entails the imitation theory of
     art: the poem must be regarded as symbolic. See also
     "The Object of the Poem" (C67).

C76 "Mr. Leavis on D.H. Lawrence." Review of Leavis, F.R.,
     D.H. Lawrence: Novelist. The Sewanee Review 65, 1
     (January, 1957), pp. 123-36.

     Attacks Leavis' reverential attitude toward Lawrence
     that blinds him to Lawrence's flaws and creates an out-
     of-focus perspective of that novelist's work. Specifi-
     cally, Leavis' "failure to follow Lawrence's injunction
     to trust the tale leads him to miss how the didactic will
     of the writer functions in it." Vivas takes the reader

into several of Lawrence's "poems" to show that his
triumphs were accompanied by frequent failures and it is
only by acknowledging the latter that one can fully ap-
preciate the former.

Leavis is faulted for lack of critical theory and anti-
pathy to philosophy. Vivas vehemently objects to Leavis'
claim that "theory blunts the sensibility" and insists
that the critic who tries to avoid theory "ends up with
many theories, and the upshot cannot but be incoherence."
The essay goes on to show how this is true in the case
of "the principles that guide Mr. Leavis' criticism."

Of concern, also, is Leavis' method of criticism which
consists largely of "extensive paraphrases accompanied by
frequent and long quotations with indications of values
to be discerned." This results in Leavis' inability to
provide the "key" to the organization of such works as
Women in Love, and his tendency to cover up his lack of
theory with technical terms such as "presentment" and
"vacuous generalizations" that turn out, on inspection,
to be "colossal oversimplifications." (See also C55.)

C77   "Four Meanings of 'Education.'" *Papers and Studies* (a
      pamphlet). The Institute for Christian Learning (Feb-
      ruary, 1958), 16 pp.

Dwells at length on the third and fourth of four meanings of education after noting that "education" might
mean either "enculturation" or "the training of the mind."
Vivas prefers to think of education as "something that
happens to a mind when it awakes to the need to assimilate
the spiritual and the intellectual heritage of our civilization," or to think of education as roughly equivalent
to "vocation," when a person discovers the "person he
truly is or needs to become," which he designates the
word's fourth meaning. Throughout Vivas emphasizes that
education is not learning and a scholar is not a prototype
of the educated person.

C78   "The Two Lawrences." *Bucknell Review* 7, 3 (March, 1958),
      pp. 113-32.

The first chapter of Vivas' book on Lawrence, which will
appear in 1960, this essay differentiates between Lawrence
the man of muddled thought, and Lawrence the poet of
occasional genius. It develops Lawrence's comment about
the novel: "Oh give me the novel. Let me hear what the
novel says. As for the novelist, he is usually a dribbling
liar"; and shows how Lawrence himself fought, at times

unsuccessfully, against "that bullying passion and auto-
cratic ideology" rather than being able to "digest his
experience aesthetically." The failure in Lawrence's art
is marked by such a loss of control, whereas his triumph
comes about when he is able, as he is in *Women in Love*,
The Rainbow, and *Sons and Lovers*, to achieve "pure
poetry."

C79   "The Substance of *Women in Love*." *The Sewanee Review*
        66, 1 (Autumn, 1958), pp. 588-632.

Focuses on one of Lawrence's "triumphs" by showing how
Lawrence "transformed" the matter of his experience into
the "substance" of his novel. Vivas argues that Lawrence
approaches the novel from within the bosom of "atheistic
existentialism" to wrestle with the problem of human
destiny and the failure of religion in the modern world.
But Lawrence's transformation succeeds because he is able
to present the problem in dramatic terms. Gerald Crich,
for example, "is a person grasped directly, not in terms
of concepts, a moving, responding, human being...."
Vivas carefully distinguishes the aesthetic mode of
apprehension, which is direct, dramatic, and primarily
imaginative, from the nonaesthetic discursive, "transi-
tive," or reflective and conceptual mode of apprehension.
In part, Lawrence achieves his end by the use of constitutive symbols (see the introduction), which require direct
and immediate communion between object and spectator and
cannot be "explained" in discursive language; they can
only be displayed dramatically. If there is "truth" in
literature it is here, on this level, that it will be
found, and not on the abstract level of the philosopher.
The novelist purchases vivid presentation at the price of
systematic completeness.

C80   "Mi ritrovai per una selva oscura." *The Sewanee Review*
        67, 4 (Autumn, 1959), pp. 560-6.

Pays tribute to Allen Tate as one who helped Vivas find
his way when he was "lost in a dark wood" of error. Shows
how Tate's *Reactionary Essays* helped to mould Vivas'
commitment to new criticism as housing those critics "who
take literature seriously."

C81   "The Tragic Dimension." Review of Sewall, Richard B.,
       The Vision of Tragedy, and Levin, Harry, *The Question
       of Hamlet*. *The Yale Review* 48, 4 (June, 1959), pp.
       587-93.

       Exhibits high praise for Sewall's book as one that con-
       cerns itself with "the tragic dimension of human experi-
       ence," after an extended critique of the "Neo-Aristotelians
       of Chicago" and their attempts to reduce tragedy to a
       problem of classification. References suggest that it is
       in Sewall's work that Vivas found the germ for his notion
       of "unmitigated tragedies" (see C114 and C119). Alludes
       to his desertion of naturalism and the new-found tragic
       theory of the naturalists that reduces tragedy to pathos.
       The Levin book provides Vivas with the opportunity to
       argue that too much learning can interfere with a man's
       reading of a play--if that reading is to be revelatory of
       what the poet is trying to say. Vivas argues that *Hamlet*
       is not an "integrated" poem but, rather, "a something or
       several somethings." Suggests the view that art is funda-
       mentally ambiguous, when regarded from a conceptual point
       of view.

C82   "Contextualism Reconsidered." *The Journal of Aesthetics
       & Art Criticism* 18, 2 (December, 1959), pp. 222-40.

       Responds to Walter Sutton's criticisms of "contextual-
       ism" (see G38 and G39) which amount to a denial of the
       "residential" function of poetry. Vivas stresses the
       primacy of the aesthetic: life imitates art and not the
       other way 'round. In addition, Vivas denies that language
       need be referential since it "performs a large number of
       functions." What the language of poetry does is to
       "allow us to grasp reality, without which no referential
       use of language is possible." In other words, the refer-
       ential use of language is derivative; its primary use is
       poetic. The remainder of the essay is given over to a
       detailed response to Sutton's denial of the "intransitive"
       nature of aesthetic experience. While Vivas acknowledges
       that true aesthetic experience is rare, he insists that
       it does occur, and because of this, he still has "good
       grounds for arguing that the definition would retain its
       utility." Of central importance to his definition is his
       distinction between emotion and feeling: the former, as
       self-conscious, is absent from the aesthetic experience,
       the latter is present. (See also "A Definition of the
       Aesthetic Experience," C20.)

C82a   "Contextualism Reconsidered." *The Artistic Trans-
       action* (A4), pp. 171-202.

       Reprint of C82.

C83 "Creativity in Art and Education." *The Arts Symposium on
     the Creative Process*. Randolph-Macon Women's College
     (March, 1960).

     Uses anthropological evidence from Franz Boas to estab-
     lish his thesis that the end of art is not pleasure, but
     the expression of a fundamental human need. Concludes
     with a discussion of the place of creativity in education
     "in all of its three meanings." Creativity is involved
     in education in the sense of enculturation, the acquisi-
     tion of knowledge, and the taking over of culture. (See
     also C77.)

C83a   "Creativity in Art and Education." *Teachers'
       College Record* 62, 2 (November, 1960), pp. 140-8.

       Reprint of C83.

C84 "In Defense of Non-Objective Art." *Modern Age* 4, 4
     (Fall, 1960), pp. 412-5.

     A rejoinder to Geoffrey Wagner's essay "The Organized
     Heresy: Abstract Art in the United States" (Summer, 1960,
     issue of *Modern Age*). Responds to what seems a reaction
     on Mr. Wagner's part to non-objective art, on the grounds
     that there can be no orthodox, and therefore no heretical,
     art. "To dismiss non-objectivist art in anger," Vivas
     writes, "is to neglect something of great importance to
     anyone seeking to understand our culture." Argues for
     the autonomy of art and the artist, and distinguishes
     non-objective art from objective art in that it is a means
     of grasping "what, in one of Santayana's happy phrases,
     we may call the inward landscape," with all its brutality,
     violence, and hatred. "It has much more of the id in it
     than Ingres put into his figures."

C84a   "In Defense of Non-Objective Art." *The Artistic
       Transaction* (A4), pp. 142-51.

       Reprint of C84.

C85 "Science and the Studies of Man." Schoeck, Helmut, and
     Wiggins, James W., eds., *Scientism and Values*. Prince-
     ton: D. Van Nostrand Company, 1960, pp. 50-82.

     Attacks the "behavioral sciences" on the grounds that
     they are a form of "scientism"--the uncritical claim that

such studies have the status of science, or that the
scientific method is the only reliable method to approach
knowledge. Of major concern is the behaviorist's denial
of value on the grounds of the absence of proof, in the
narrow sense, that value is a part of the real world.
Expresses the view, expanded more fully in *Two Roads to
Ignorance* (pp. 193ff.), that the naturalistic conviction
of the self-sufficiency of their methods is a matter of
faith.

C86 "Freedom: The Philosophical Problem." *Modern Age* 6, 1
     (Winter, 1961), pp. 7-20.

     Rejects the deterministic hypothesis of scientistic
naturalism as empirically unfounded. Defends "philosophical freedom," or the view that man is self-determined or
autonomous (as Kant would have it). The problem of freedom must not be addressed as an abstract problem, since
we are "always to some extent determined by culture,"
and therefore "freedom is always freedom within a web of
determinations."
     Freedom is a necessary presupposition of morality, but
subjective feeling is not sufficient evidence of freedom.
The phenomenon of human creativity--its fundamental
mystery--is, however, adequate basis for the hypothesis
that we are free. "Further, the hypothesis of radical
creativity gives me a better picture of the universe than
I can get without it."

     C86a "Freedom: The Philosophical Problem." Morley,
           Felix, ed., *The Necessary Conditions of a Free
           Society*. Princeton: D. Van Nostrand Co., 1963,
           pp. 120-41.

           Reprint of C86.

C87 "Animadversions on Imitation and Expression." *The Journal
     of Aesthetics and Art Criticism* 19, 4 (Summer, 1961),
     pp. 425-32.

     Contains a lengthy examination and defense of the mystery
of human creation, as against those who think of art as
imitation or the expression of emotion. Suggests the
substitution of "contextual coherence" for Aristotle's
notion of "probability." It is precisely contextual coherence that makes the intransitive experience possible.
Aristotle's notions of imitation and probability suggest
references outside the poem, whereas (in the case of a
story such as Kafka's *Metamorphosis*) "the story is self-
sufficient, autonomous, and its autonomy or self-suffi-

ciency forces us, the readers, to stay within its universe,
to read it intransitively. We have nothing to compare it
with. And in the world of the story, the ordinary laws of
reality have no authority. The work of art makes its own
laws, and enforces them, by the isolation it imposes on
the spectator." Vivas goes so far as to suggest that
Aristotle's notion of "likely improbability" actually
suggests the principle of intransitive attention, but that
he never followed it up. At the very least "the notion of
likely improbability is incompatible with the rest of
[Aristotle's] theory."

Expression theories are "but disguised theories of imitation," as Vivas has shown in "The Objective Correlative
of T.S. Eliot" (C46), and suffer from the same defects.
In the case of Susanne Langer's work in aesthetics, for
instance, art is considered to be an imitation "of the
dynamics of subjective experience," though Langer adds a
distinction between "arousal of emotion in the reader by
the object of art and the expression of the emotion by it."
Thus Vivas adds to his criticisms of the expression theory
several considerations that apply to Langer's version of
that theory. Briefly put, Vivas contends that Langer's
view commits her to the claim that affective experience is
structured and this claim is suspect; in addition, her view
obscures the problem since the structure of the work of
art is more accessible than the structure of an emotional
response to that work.

In the end, expression theories of art fail because the
term "expression" fails to convey what it is that the
artist does, "if the function of art is expression, art
is something for which at least one substitute--psychic
therapy--can be found." It may be that expression is one
(non-residential) function of art, but it cannot be regarded as its main function.

C87a "Animadversions on Imitation and Expression." *The*
        Artistic Transaction (A4), pp. 153-68.

        Reprint of C87.

C88 "Metaphysics for 632 A.F." Review of Brown, Norman O.,
        Life Against Death. The Sewanee Review 69, 4 (October,
        1961), pp. 677-90.

        Contrasts Brown's book with Marcuse's *Eros and Civiliza-*
        tion and finds it more compelling and more radical in its
        condemnation of contemporary civilization. What is needed,
        according to Brown, is a "radical upheaval, one that would
        jettison those values we have hitherto considered the

highest." After a brief summary of Brown's book Vivas
attacks the very loose usage of terms such as "instinct"
and "mental energy" as substituting "one mystery for
another." They are "figleaf terms" that we have invented
to cover "our shame and ignorance." Also under attack is
Brown's reductionism, the rejection of non-material enti-
ties *tout court*, despite his admission that "we need ...
a metaphysic which recognizes both the continuity between
man and animals and also the discontinuity."

Vivas anticipates his extended critique of psychological
hedonism, in *Contra Marcuse*, as based on a simplistic
collapsing of the difference between the by-product of a
drive (pleasure) and the object of the drive: the fact
that Jones derives pleasure from doing his duty does not
imply that this pleasure was his goal in choosing to do
his duty. Brown goes beyond psychological hedonism, however, to ethical hedonism, to the view that one *ought* to
pursue pleasure. Vivas objects that the eradication of
restraint in "pure pleasure" would result in the eradication of culture and a less-than-human existence. One
might add that ethical hedonism makes no sense when based
on psychological hedonism--if one *does*, in fact, pursue
pleasure, it makes no sense to say that he *ought* to do so.

C89 "Reiterations and Second Thoughts on Cultural Relativism."
     Schoeck, Helmut, and Wiggins, James W., eds., *Relativism
     and the Study of Man*. Princeton: D. Van Nostrand Co.,
     1961, pp. 45-73.

     Argues against the view that values are simply products
     of enculturation on the grounds that cross-cultural value
     judgments are possible, as are criticisms of a particular
     culture's values from within that culture. Generally, a
     culture's values, including our own, are measured by how
     fully they help to develop "human capacities." Relativism
     is a pernicious doctrine, especially at a time when "the
     pressing political need is to find a way of mediating
     differences among peoples."

C90 "Art and the Artist's 'Citizenship.'" *Modern Age* 6, 1
     (Spring, 1962), pp. 155-64.

     Defines art as the "capacity to grasp the furniture of
     the world by means of symbols," and argues that art, and
     the artist, are autonomous. Expresses concern over the
     increasing "encroachment" by the state and its institu-
     tions upon the artist's privacy.

C90a "Art and the Artist's Citizenship." Schoeck,
      Helmut, and Wiggins, James W., eds., *The New
      Argument in Economics: The Public Versus the
      Private Sector*. Princeton: D. Van Nostrand Co.,
      1963, pp. 120-41.

      Reprint of C90.

C91 "Relativism: Its Paradoxes and Pitfalls." Intercollegiate
      Society of Individualists, Philadelphia, Pennsylvania
      (October, 1962), p. 19.

      Argues that relativism is a "pernicious doctrine,"
      because it teaches that since all values are relative
      "one pattern of values is as good as another." Relativism
      fails to distinguish between our knowledge of value and
      the being of value. Our knowledge of value may be rela-
      tive, but it does not follow from this that the values
      themselves are relative. Because values are not relative,
      cross-cultural value judgments are possible and it is
      also possible to judge diverse cultures in accordance
      with the degree of human "development" they permit. The
      denial of relativism does not entail "absolutism" (on
      this point, see Chapter XVII of *Two Roads to Ignorance*
      (A6) and C89 above).

C92 "The Liberal Ethos." Review of Toledano, Ralph de,
      Seeds of Treason. *Modern Age* 7, 2 (Spring, 1963),
      pp. 206-10.

      Attempts to grasp the significance of the "Seeds of
      Treason"--especially with regard to the trial of Alger
      Hiss--with an eye to seeing how they reflect the "dominant
      ethos of our society."

C93 "Narcissists and Others." Review of Peyre, Henri,
      Literature and Sincerity. *The Yale Review* 57, 4
      (June, 1963), pp. 617-22.

      Generally favorable comments about the book precede an
      examination of Peyre's discussion of "literary sincerity."
      Faults the book for failure to come to terms with that
      concept after initial indications were that it would
      explain it fully.

C94 "The Revolution in Personal Values," Reid, T.E.H., ed.,
      Values in Conflict. Toronto: University of Toronto
      Press, 1963, pp. 92-111.

      Argues, at some length, that the present crisis in
      values is a conflict within the individual as well as

a conflict in the world. The individual conflict results
in profound ambivalence, while the crisis in values, writ
large, constitutes a denial of their reality. There
follows a most interesting defense of realism, à la Charles
Peirce. As over against the prevailing nominalism of
contemporary Anglo-American philosophy and culture, Vivas
defends the value of the Person as a necessary presupposi-
tion of morality. "Deny [the value of the Person] seriously, push the denial to the logical extreme ... and you end
up with the systematic elimination of those that the
bureaucrat in cahoots with the technical expert decides
to eliminate: Those declared to be subhuman, and those
marked as unfit by the bleeding hearts of the agents of
the top commissar."

Contains a lengthy analysis of the impact of Darwin and
Freud—especially the latter—on contemporary civilization,
which is tending, increasingly, to replace spiritual
values with material ones, a result perhaps of "the change
in our Western civilization from a dominantly sacramental
culture into an increasingly secular one...."

C95 "Literature and Ideology." *The Artistic Transaction* (A4),
      pp. 95-116.

A revised version of the Alumni Fund Lecture at Northwestern University on April 27, 1960 (E6), which appears
in print for the first time here. Develops at some length
the difference between dramatic presentation and dramatized concepts. The first is art, the second is ideology.
"The artist solves no problems, he answers no questions....
Literature on the aesthetic that controls this essay, is
inherently and ineradicably ambiguous."

C96 "The Substance of Tragedy." *The Artistic Transaction*
      (A4), pp. 117-40.

Examines *Antigone* and *King Lear* from the point of view
of the "matter that is informed into poetic substance."
Suggests some of the themes developed later in his view
of "unmitigated" tragedy (see C114 and C119), the "in-
volvement of a flawed man with a flawed cosmos."

C97 "Some Notes on Truth." *The Personalist* 45, 2 (Spring,
      1964), pp. 176-92.

Defends the view that the phrase "objective truth" is
pleonastic, as against those of his contemporaries who
argue that truth is subjective and philosophy mere biography. Examines several possible meanings of the phrase
"subjective truth" and rejects each as untenable.

C97a   "Notes on Truth." *Philosophy Today* 8, 1-4 (Spring,
        1964), pp. 46-55.

        Reprint of C97.

C98   "On the Conservative Demonology." *Modern Age* 8, 2
       (Spring, 1964), pp. 119-33.

       Defends the role of the "devils," Marx and Freud, in
       the Conservative movement. Contends that every movement
       requires its devils alongside its patron saints and holy
       men. Conservatism has such men in Burke, Irving Babbitt,
       Russell Kirk, and William Buckley. If conservatism is
       to have an impact on Western civilization, according to
       Vivas, it will have to "develop a philosophy that is
       systematic, that is comprehensive, that takes full and
       honest account of current positive knowledge and that is,
       therefore, no mere repetition of dried up old chestnuts
       that appealed to men a generation or two ago, but have
       lost their flavor and freshness." Defends the value of
       Truth as the paramount value in the American panoply of
       values and argues that it is in defense of this value
       that the demons must be defended.

C99   "The Mind of Richard Weaver." Review of Weaver, Richard,
       Visions of Order. *Modern Age* 8, 3 (Spring, 1964),
       pp. 307-10.

       Weighs the strengths and weaknesses of Weaver's book
       in terms generally filled with praise, but expresses
       regret over Weaver's equivocal use of the term "culture."
       Distinguishes, in this regard, between the "sociological"
       and the "honorific" sense of this term and insists that
       it is in the latter sense that "human groups pursue
       values and accept meanings that enable them not only to
       survive but to give some worth to their lives."

C100   "The Self and Its Masks." *The Southern Review* 1, 2
       (Spring, 1965), pp. 317-36.

       Explores the differences between the discursive sci-
       ences, chiefly psychology, and poetry in their attempts
       to come to know human beings. Argues that the psychol-
       ogist cannot know all there is to know about persons
       because of the masks persons wear, but that the poet can
       penetrate their masks, on occasion, because of his ability
       to perceive creatively; and the "aesthetic mode of ex-
       perience has the primacy over all other modes." The poet
       does not provide us with knowledge, however, as Vivas
       insists throughout his work. Rather, he provides us

with the "dramatic-moral categories through which we
grasp the world in which we live."

In short, the world cannot do without literature
because "the grasp of the world that literature gives
us is one for which we can find no substitute in the
works of the scientists, not even Freud."

C101 "Things and Persons." *Modern Age* 9, 2 (Spring, 1965),
pp. 119-31.

Expands the concept of the "person" as put forth in
The Moral Life and the Ethical Life (A1). Argues that
"person" is a normative term and not to be defined by
social science: persons have intrinsic worth, a worth
that is "indefeasible, ineradicable, irrefragable, and
inviolable." This applies to all persons no matter how
despicable they are, as the denial of the worth of any
person involves a doctrine of the "systematic elimination of those [you] hold to be inferior." To the end,
it is the person's capacity to discover value that comprises the basis for the inviolability of personhood.
The argument for his claim is made by a lengthy contrast
between persons and things.

C102 "Dostoevsky: Philosopher or Novelist?" Review of
Wasiolek, Edward, *Dostoevsky: The Major Fiction.*
Modern Age 9, 3 (Summer, 1965), pp. 302-9.

Argues, *contra* Wasiolek, that the novelist does not
work ideas into his novels the way a cook works egg
whites into batter. It is a mistake to insist that
"Dostoevsky first thought out his problems in the way
in which philosophers think theirs and then 'dramatized'
his thought." Dostoevsky's particular genius was his
ability to suspend his philosophical and theological
judgment during the creation of his works of art. (See
also "Dostoevsky, 'Poet' in Spite of Himself," C124).
Novelists think "concretely and not abstractly" and
Dostoevsky was, above all else, a novelist *par excellence.*

C103 "Apologia Pro Fide Mea." *Intercollegiate Review* 2, 2
(October, 1965), pp. 126-37.

An "apology" for Vivas' conservative philosophy that
contains an interesting analysis of the terms "conservative" and "liberal." Locates the main difference between the two in the acceptance of the inevitability of
evil by the former and the naive hope on the part of the
latter that it can be eradicated by social engineering.

The difference is critical since Vivas, following
Nietzsche and Dostoevsky, insists that the liberals, or
socialists, "think men are slaves and are prepared to
treat them as such," whereas conservatives "think men
have a metaphysical dimension, of which freedom is a
component, and we are prepared to pay the price freedom
exacts, lest we turn men into cattle."

C104   Introduction to Weaver, Richard, *Life Without Prejudice,*
        and Other Essays. Chicago: Henry Regnery Co., 1965,
        pp. vii–xvii.

A tribute to Richard Weaver on the occasion of the
publication of a posthumous collection of his essays by
Harvey Plotnick.

C105   Introduction to Nietzsche, Friedrich, *Schopenhauer as*
        Educator, trans. Hillesheim, James W., and Simpson,
        Malcolm B. Chicago: Henry Regnery Co., Gateway
        Editions, 1965, pp. vii–xx.

Points out that Nietzsche's essay is less about
Schopenhauer and more about Nietzsche—and especially
about Nietzsche's early educational philosophy. Expounds
on the difference between training and education as he
had done in "Four Meanings of 'Education'" (C77) and
insists that by and large the Anglo-American "Establish-
ment" has confused the latter with the former. Nietzsche
did not confuse the two and was acutely aware that
education involves "liberation" and that this is a rare
event.

C106   "Were They Radicals or Intellectuals?" Review of Lasch,
        Christopher, *The New Radicalism in America.* *The Inter-*
        collegiate Review 2, 4 (January, 1966), pp. 251–60.

Strongly disagrees with Lasch that intellectuals, in
general, are of little influence on the seat of power.
Contrariwise, their impact results from their ability
to create doctrine, "finding and speeding its spread."
The "radicals" discussed in this book, and others like
them, have been responsible for "changing the nation's
ethos from a conservative, nationalistic, moral one to
a socialistic, antipatriotic, amoral one." Argues with
vehemence that the author is naive in his view of who
it is that preserves and destroys values.

C107 "Animadversions Upon the Doctrine of Natural Law."
      Modern Age 10, 2 (Spring, 1966), pp. 149-60.

      Examines the grounds for rejecting "the doctrine of
      Natural Law" and suggests the alternative of axiological
      realism as "more adequate to moral experience than
      notions of natural moral law and more in harmony with
      what we know--or perhaps it were better to say what we
      do not know--about the universe, than the hypothesis of
      natural law."

C108 "Philosophy of Culture, Aesthetics and Criticism: Some
      Problems." *Texas Quarterly* 9, 1 (Spring, 1966), pp.
      231-41.

      Argues that because of art's inherent ambiguity there
      can be no one "exclusively right theory of criticism and
      therefore [no] one exclusively right set of practical
      comments that can be made about a work of art." The
      only way this view avoids relativism is by analyzing the
      various modes of human experience, moral, religious,
      cognitive, and aesthetic, that comprise culture. The
      various modes of experience are impure, they blend with
      one another, the aesthetic mode easily passes over into
      the cognitive or the religious. The function of criti-
      cism, therefore, is to dismiss those responses that are
      clearly non-aesthetic and to focus attention on those
      "legitimate" responses that are as singularly aesthetic
      as possible. This dictum allows us to dismiss those
      critics who are unwilling or unable to "take literature
      seriously" *as* literature, as an aesthetic object, and
      insist upon reading it as sociological, psychological,
      or historical documents. We must insist upon the
      distinction between the subject matter of the poem and
      the substance of the poem and insist also that the
      critic focus attention on the meanings and values that
      constitute the latter, the poem that "holds us in its
      power."

      C108a "Filosofia della cultura, estetica e critica:
             alcuni problema." *Op. cit., selezione della
             critica d'arte contemporanea* (Naples, Italy).
             Maggio, 1967, #9.

             Translation of C108.

C109 "Reply to Some Criticisms." *Criticism: A Survey of
      Literature and Arts* 9, 2 (Spring, 1967), pp. 123-41.

      Responds to W.K. Wimsatt's review article on *The
      Artistic Transaction* (see G44) by defending his claim

that the self-sufficiency and untranslatability of a
poem can only be explained by reference to its "immanent"
meaning (its residential aspect). The key issue is the
following: what can art do, and to a lesser extent what
does it do, that no other human activity does? Vivas'
response is that it creates culture by providing what
Joseph Wood Krutch called "the categories of perception
and forms of feeling" by means of which we grasp the
external and internal world. Contains several brief
phenomenological descriptions of aesthetic objects that
help to shed light on Vivas' contention that the aesthetic
mode of apprehension is *sui generis* and concludes with
several brief words about reviews of his book by Carl
Hausman and Angelo Bertocci. This last contains a clari-
fication of Vivas' notion of the "constitutive symbol"
and its relation to the various modes of experience that
comprise "culture."

C110 Introduction to Freud, Sigmund, *The Origin and Develop-*
         ment of Psychoanalysis. Chicago: Henry Regnery Co.,
         Gateway Editions, 1967, pp. v-xxxv.

Expresses generally high praise for Freud's "philosophical" views, while at the same time discounting much of
their scientific status--though the praise is not without
qualification. Vivas would reject Freud's materialism,
or his naturalism, which entails the denial of specifically human status to *homo sapiens*, though he thinks that
Freud's thinking provides a challenge to other natural-
ists--and to philosophers as well, who have tended to
ignore what Freud had to say.

C111 "Is a Conservative Anthropology Possible?" *Social*
         Research 35, 4 (Winter, 1968), pp. 593-615.

Examines the degree to which science is subjective or
ideological. Suggests that as knowledge, scientific
truth is neither "partisan" nor subjective except to
the extent--as per Polanyi--that subjective factors
enter into the acquisition of knowledge. Questions the
extent to which the social sciences are scientific, and
therefore non-ideological and objective, by focusing on
a number of unquestioned presuppositions that permeate
the social sciences. Among these are found "cultural
relativity," and the assumption of equality of aptitude
among different races of men. Concludes that the social
sciences are more thoroughly ideological than many social
scientists might readily admit.

C112 "Literary Classes: Some Problems." *Genre* 1, 2 (April, 1968), pp. 97-105.

Traces the reasons for the rejection of genres from an aesthetic, philosophical, and sociological perspective. Aesthetically, poets and artists reject the old forms as unsuitable for the new matter they seek to present. Socially, the artist cannot count on a "homogeneously educated audience." As a result, the artist is freer, less constrained, though this is not an unqualified good since it gives to "originality the primacy among his values as artist." Philosophically, the rejection of classes is a result of a pervasive nominalism and the assumption that classes are mere conventions. Vivas defends the notion of genres on the basis of their utility: while classifications can readily be abused (as in the case of the neo-Aristotelians) they are nonetheless indispensable to the theorist who seeks an understanding of the work to be examined. In short: "The poet works within a tradition. What he contributes to it modifies it. But he cannot step out of a tradition." And if one seeks to grasp the poet's work without concepts, cate-gories, or theory he must necessarily flounder. (See C55, C117, and C128.) "Anyone who engages in criticism without logically sterilized theoretical tools spreads the gangrene of confusion."

C113 "A Good Guy or a Bad One." Review of Pear, D.F., *Bertrand Russell and the British Tradition*, and Adler, Mortimer, *The Defense of Man and the Difference It Makes*. *Modern Age* 12, 2 (Spring, 1968), pp. 174-82.

Distinguishes among four different "Russells" from which Mr. Pear has chosen to expound the views of one, the "technical" Russell. Praises the book as an exercise in technical philosophy, but is critical of the man Russell who was wont to "throw his weight around because his moral passions are better than those who in his country and ours carry the heavy burden of managing their affairs." Acknowledges the man's genius while expressing concern over the "incongruous combination of genius and imbecility."
Expresses generally high praise for Adler's book as one that faces a problem squarely in the true spirit of philosophy, and is generally high in praise of Adler himself for having the courage to "swim against the [academic] current." Charges are pressed against philoso-phers generally for the hypocrisy they have shown toward

such "operators" as Adler. The essay is a study in
contrasts between the two men and the acceptance or
the rejection they have received from their peers.

C114   "Atrabilious Thoughts on a Theory of Tragedy." Knauf,
       David M., ed., *Papers in Dramatic Theory and Criticism*.
       Iowa City: University of Iowa Press, 1969, pp. 9-23.

       Attacks the "moralistic interpretation of tragedy"
       by contending that there are a few "unmitigated" tragedies,
       plays that reveal a flaw in being. In these plays, *The
       Oresteia*, for example, we witness "unmerited catastrophe"
       that cannot be explained away. (See also "Tragedy and
       the Broader Consciousness," C119.)

C115   "Myth: Some Philosophical Problems." *Southern Review*
       6, 1 (Winter 1970), pp. 89-103.

       Insists upon modern man's need for myth despite his
       presumed sophistication. "The assumption that men can
       live without myth is one of the precious 'truths' of
       village atheists and vestigial eighteenth-century ration-
       alists living in mid-century...." But while the need
       for myth is beyond question, the nature of its rôle needs
       to be examined. Myth does not provide knowledge, though
       it is not unrelated to knowledge: myth is fundamentally
       symbolic and functions as does art to help us grasp our
       world.
       Contrasts our mythic pictures of the world with our
       scientific pictures. Each is "adequate" in different
       senses of this term, since each fills a different human
       need. Science cannot replace myth, especially religious
       myth, since the latter attests to the fact of mystery
       in the world which the former denies.

C116   "Reality in Literature." *Iowa Review* 1, 4 (Fall, 1970),
       pp. 116-27.

       Provides an excellent overview of Vivas' aesthetic
       theory together with an extended discussion of what he
       means when he says that "the poem is a complicated tissue
       of meanings and values expressed in and through [its]
       language."
       Links this explanation with an examination of the
       distinction between signs and symbols. It is because
       the poet employs the latter that his poetry is untrans-
       latable and cannot be satisfactorily paraphrased.

C117 "Literary Criticism and Aesthetics." Scholes, Robert, ed., *Philosopher Critic*. Tulsa: University of Tulsa Press, 1970, pp. 18-39.

Argues that the new criticism arose in opposition to impressionistic, moralistic, and Marxist criticism but that it succumbed in the end because of a lack of "men theoretically equipped to meet the challenges of their opponents." In the end the new criticism comprised "a brilliant interlude between, on the one hand the twenties, the era of impressionism, the New Humanism, the decade of the commissars, and on the other the reactionary debility of the epigones of our own day."

Lists the charges against the new criticism by the historicists and journalists but insists that the new criticism suffered most by its own absence of theory, a claim which is elaborated by means of an examination of the relation between theory and practical criticism. "The choice is not between sensibility and principles. It is between a sensibility that is informed--explicitly or implicitly--by lucid and coherent principles and one that is not."

To increase the muddle, aesthetics (and aestheticians) have little or nothing to do with practical criticism and so the gulf between the two widens. As a result, both aesthetics and criticism suffer. "There is need of a satisfactory apologia for the arts and for our interest in them, and we also need a true account of the dignity of the objects with which we are professionally concerned. The need is urgent."

In an appendix attached to the essay, Vivas briefly examines several new books in criticism to see whether he needs to adjust his thinking in light of their revelations. He discusses William Righter's *Logic and Criticism*, John Casey's *The Language of Criticism*, and E.D. Hirsch's *Validity in Interpretation*. Although he praises elements of Hirsch's book, he finds in none of the three grounds for rejection of his basic contention. The need for an "apologia" is still "urgent."

C118 "Marcuse as Torquemada of the Left." *The New York Times* (June 15, 1971), p. 43.

Expresses concern over Marcuse's "aprioristic disregard of empirical data; the frozen certainty about open questions; in some crucial respects, its shallowness and its incoherence [referring to Marcuse's rhetoric generally]." Generally reviews several points developed earlier in *Contra Marcuse* (A5).

C119   "Tragedy and the Broader Consciousness." *Southern
          Review* 7, 3 (Summer 1971), pp. 846-65.

        Returns to the subject of "unmitigated" tragedy (see
   C114) with a detailed examination of *King Lear* as an
   example (one of the very few) of a play whose substance
   reveals a flaw in being. This tragedy, like the *Oresteia*,
   demonstrates this because "it presents an action that,
   to our sense of equity, reaches the extreme limit of
   sheer gratuitous or arbitrarily ordained catastrophe."
   The "transcendent evil" that is revealed in *King Lear*,
   "evil so utterly uncalled for," grounds Vivas' conservatism and provides the link between his conservatism and
   his philosophy of art (see C96).

C120   Review of Stein, George P., *The Ways of Meaning in the
          Arts. The Journal of Aesthetics and Art Criticism* 30,
          1 (Fall, 1971), pp. 117-20.

        Objects to Stein's claim that meaning in art can be
   "explored without reference to a definition of art and
   a specification of the kind of response that, given the
   definition, turns an object into a work of art." Examines
   in some detail what it is that makes an object a work of
   art, and what it is that can be called "the aesthetic
   component." Contends that these questions cannot be
   satisfactorily dealt with unless one acknowledges the
   "constitutive activity of the mind," and, in the end,
   Vivas objects to Stein's confusion between the residential
   (intrinsic) and the nonresidential (extrinsic) functions
   of art.

C121   "In the Presence of Art." *Symposium Humanities* 1, 1
          (Winter, 1972), pp. 85-106.

        Contains an excellent extended description of the
   aesthetic experience and elaborates on the claim that
   the critic must attend to the values and meanings he
   finds in the work, rather than those he might bring to
   the work.
        Admits that his view of art is "restrictive" in that
   it must argue, for example, that to the extent that a
   satirical work succeeds as art it fails as satire--since
   we lose sight of the referential meaning of the work in
   rapt intransitive attention.

C122   "In Memoriam: Frank Meyer." *Modern Age* 16, 3 (Summer,
          1972), pp. 312-3.

        A tribute to Frank Meyer read at the National Meeting
   of the Philadelphia Society in Chicago on April 15, 1972.

C123 "'Poetry' and Philosophy." *The Iowa Review* 4, 3 (Summer, 1973), pp. 114-26.

Revisits the contentions of "Literature and Knowledge" (C64) in an attempt to make the thesis more "intelligible." In doing so, the concepts "poetry" and "philosophy" are carefully delineated as forms of immediate and mediate apprehension, respectively. Poetry does not yield knowledge or truth in any strict sense of these terms, since both knowledge and truth are reflective, cognitive, and systematic while the poem is none of these.

C124 "Dostoevsky, 'Poet' in Spite of Himself." *The Southern Review* 10, 2 (April, 1974), pp. 307-28.

Distinguishes carefully between Dostoevsky the man who was "anxious to express ideas" and Dostoevsky the poet who found himself--in *The Possessed*--writing a poem "in spite of himself." Develops the view expressed earlier ("Dostoevsky: Philosopher or Novelist?" C102) that the novelist performs a "genuine synthesis" and as such the poem "neither defends nor attacks, proves nor disproves, ... it merely presents."

Contains an excellent discussion of "The Grand Inquisitor" as a "sequel to" the two preceding chapters in the novel--which Vivas dubs "Ivan's Dossier." In this section of the novel, we find a dramatic presentation of the choice confronting mankind: freedom or bread. It is important to note that this is a dramatic presentation and not a philosophical or theological response. As such it is irreducibly ambiguous. "We cannot overlook the ambiguity of the poem." As Alyosha points out to Ivan, "your poem is in praise of Jesus, not in blame of Him--as you mean it to be!" This is precisely what the distinction between the man and the poet entails: "one or the other or both may be wrong about what the poet actually accomplishes."

C125 "On Aesthetics and Jung." *Modern Age* 18, 3 (Summer, 1974), pp. 246-56.

Sketches an aesthetic that is in agreement with Jung's view of art in an attempt to show that Jung's analytical psychology throws important light on "the phenomenon of art." This is particularly true of the light the archetype throws on the experience of catharsis. The archetypes in Vivas' view comprise part of the "matter" of experience to be transformed by the artist in creating a work of art. The cathartic effect of the archetypes

is an aspect of the non-residential function of art—an
improvement over Aristotle's view, since it allows for
a greater variety of responses to art than simply pity
and fear. The primary, residential function of art is
to present meanings and values.

C126   "Teachers and 'Teachers.'" *Modern Age* 19, 3 (Summer,
         1975), pp. 226-35.

The first of five chapters of *Two Roads to Ignorance*
(A6) especially reworked for *Modern Age*, this essay is
from the early, autobiographical portion of the book and
recounts Vivas' (Alonzo Quijano's) experience with
"propagandists" posing as teachers and with academic
in-fighting.

C126a   "Teachers and 'Teachers.'" *Two Roads to Ignor-*
            ance (A6).

A slightly modified and expanded version of
C126.

C127   "Alonzo as 'Teacher.'" *Modern Age* 19, 4 (Fall, 1975),
         pp. 355-63.

Picks up where the previous essay left off and describes Vivas' own attempts at teaching early on. Discusses the differences between teaching and indoctrina-
tion, and describes his early attempts at "breaking
down" his students' inherent conservatism: "substituting
one encrusted dogmatism for another, one petrified intolerance for another, one set of unreasoning prejudices
for another."

C127a   "Alonzo as 'Teacher.'" *Two Roads to Ignorance*
            (A6).

A slightly modified and expanded version of C127.

C128   "Critical Assizes." *The Blue Guitar, Rivista Annuale di*
         Letteratura Inglesa e Americana, Facultà di Magistero,
         Università di Messina, 1, 1 (1975), pp. 59-87.

Attacks an unnamed source as typical of contemporary
criticism "particularly the theories of critics that
believe no theory of criticism is necessary to practice
their trade," by reiterating his own views of aesthetics
and theory of criticism. Together with "Literary Classes"
(C112), "Literary Criticism and Aesthetics" (C117), and
"'Poetry' and Philosophy" (C123), this essay functions

as part of a rear guard action to cover the retreat of
the new criticism from the scene leaving behind various
other schools that exhibit even less proclivity for
theory. Once again, Vivas points out that what the
novelist does, qua poet, cannot be done by anyone else,
and that novels are not philosophical, sociological, or
psychological essays. Calls for critics to read literature *as literature*. While he admits that this is a
variety of "formalist" criticism, he insists that "the
formalist in literature does not ignore substance any
more than the non-formalist can ignore form."

C129 "From Left of Center to Right." *Modern Age* 20, 1
      (Winter, 1976), pp. 3-4.

      A brief note to celebrate the twentieth anniversary
      of *Modern Age*.

C130 "On Human Origins: Freud, Huxley and Malinowski."
      Modern Age 20, 2 (Spring, 1976), pp. 130-40.

      The third of five chapters from *Two Roads to Ignorance*
      (A6), the essay recounts Vivas' criticisms of the natu-
      ralistic origin of conscience and "scientistic faith"
      generally that insists, a priori, that all answers are
      to be found by proceeding in the fashion of the physicist.
      Makes the case for mystery and the inexplicable in
      questions of human origins.

      C130a "On Human Origins: Freud and Others." *Two Roads
             to Ignorance* (A6).

             A slightly expanded and modified version of C130.

C131 "The Dignity of Art." *Modern Age* 21, 3 (Summer, 1977),
      pp. 240-50.

      Responds in the affirmative to the question of whether
      the fine arts "play a part in our human living for which
      there is no substitute" by iterating Vivas' conception
      of the place of art in culture: "it is logically, but
      not temporally, prior to any kind of activity in which
      we human beings engage when we act with deliberation."

C132 "Was the Quest a Success?" *Modern Age* 21, 4 (Fall, 1977),
      pp. 354-66.

      The final two chapters from *Two Roads to Ignorance* (A6)
      combined to provide an overview of Vivas' aesthetics and
      an opportunity for "Alonzo" to reflect on a long and

sometimes painful academic career. On balance, that
career was successful, not because of the answers he has
discovered, but because "of the efforts to reach" those
answers.

C132a "Was the Quest a Failure?" *Two Roads to Ignor-
          ance* (A6).

       A brief, concluding portion of C132.

C133 "Pragmatism and the Tragic Sense of Life." *Modern Age*
          22, 3 (Summer, 1978), pp. 226-36.

       The final installment of five portions of *Two Roads
       to Ignorance* (A6), "Alonzo" recounts his attacks on the
       "banal" pragmatic view of tragedy (cf. Hook, G20) and
       his reasons for rejecting pragmatism and naturalism
       generally.

C133a "Pragmatism and the Tragic Sense of Life." *Two
          Roads to Ignorance* (A6).

       A modified and slightly expanded version of C133.

C134 "The Ethical Life." *par rapport* 1, 2 (Summer, 1978),
          pp. 77-86.

       Recounts the need to ground ethics on the concept of
       the person if we are to discover a way "to resolve moral
       perplexities morally." (See "Things and Persons," C101,
       and *The Moral Life and the Ethical Life* (A1), *passim*).
       It is only by acknowledging "ontic objectivity" and the
       status of the person that we can avoid an appeal to
       force. Provides an excellent overview of Vivas' moral
       philosophy and his axiological realism.

C135 "Two Comments on Professor Graff's Essay." *Salmagundi*
          (Summer-Fall, 1978), pp. 48-63.

       Takes Graff to task for his handling of Marcuse's
       aesthetics (in the same periodical) and Marcuse himself
       for many of the same reasons given in *Contra Marcuse*
       (A5). Argues that Graff's critique of the "presentation-
       al" view of art rests on a confusion about the nature of
       language—specifically the difference between symbols
       and signs. To a large extent, the linguistic equipment
       one requires for ordinary acts of perception is uncon-
       scious: "The act of perception includes transitive and
       intransitive perception." It is the latter that yields
       the aesthetic perception and lies at the heart of the
       artistic "presentation." Faults Graff for calling up
       the "imitation" theory of art on grounds he has stated
       elsewhere (see, for example, C87).

C136   "Poesia y cultura." *Folia Humanistica* 18 (July–August,
          1979), pp. 199–200.

          Summarizes a number of Vivas' central views of art
          and its relation to culture.

C137   "Symbols and Their Worlds." Review of Verene, Donald,
          ed., *Cassirer's Symbol, Myth and Culture. Modern Age*
          24, 1 (Winter, 1980), pp. 78–83.

          Contains an appreciative look at the value of Cassirer's
          phenomenalism and his view of man in culture. Raises
          some basic questions about Cassirer's inadequate moral
          philosophy, inadequate because it fails to provide any
          "grounds" for an *ethical* philosophy in a philosophy of
          man. Concludes with a critique of Cassirer's failure
          "to draw the implications and entailments of his theory
          of the constitutive role of the symbolic forms for his
          definition of the function of art." Shows how Vivas'
          own thinking about the place of art (and the artist)
          grows out of the shortcomings he discovers in Cassirer's
          view.

D

REVIEWS

D1 "A Chilean Mystic." Review of Mistral, Gabriela,
   Desolacion. *The Literary Review* (July 28, 1923), p. 865.

D2 "Minute Studies." Review of Holmes, Henry A.; Fierro,
   Martin; and Adams, Nicholas B., *The Romantic Dramas of
   Garcia Gutierrez*. *The Literary Review* (October 13,
   1923), p. 130.

D3 Review of Fernandez y Medina, Benjamin, *La Flor del Pago,
   Cuentos*. *The Literary Review* (November 17, 1923),
   pp. 268-9.

D4 "The Lower Depths." Review of Baroja, Pio, *Weeds*. *The
   Literary Review* (December 1, 1923), pp. 300-2.

D5 "A Spanish Impressionist." Review of Azorín (Martínez
   Ruiz, José), *Don Juan*. *The Nation* (March 19, 1924),
   p. 320.

D6 "A Spanish Play." Review of Marquina, Eduardo, and
   Fernandez Ardavin, Luis, *Rosa de Francia*. *The Literary
   Review* (March 29, 1924), p. 633.

D7 "An Old Master." Review of Allen, H. Warner, ed.,
   Celestina or The Tragicomedy of Calisto and Melibea.
   The Nation (August 6, 1924), p. 148.

D8 "A Spanish Woman Novelist." Review of Espina, Concha,
   Mariflor and the Red Beacon. *The Nation* (August 13,
   1924), p. 168.

D9 "Man's Conflicts." Review of Lawrence, D.H., *The Boy in
   the Bush*. *The New Leader* 1, 42 (November 1, 1924),
   p. 9.

D10   "Baroja Among Us." Review of Baroja, Pio, *Red Dawn*.
      New York Herald Tribune Books (November 2, 1924).

D11   "Outside the Tradition." Review of Valle Inclán, Ramón
      del, *The Pleasant Memoirs of the Marquis de Bradomin*.
      New York Herald Tribune Books (December 14, 1924).

D12   Review of Gonzales Blanco, Andreas, *Maria Jesus, Casada
      y Martir*. *The Literary Review* (1924).

D13   Review of Deakin, Frank B., *Spain Today*. *The Nation*
      (January 7, 1925), p. 21. Unsigned.

D14   "A Postil to D.H. Lawrence." Review of Lawrence, D.H.,
      The Rainbow. *The Guardian* 1, 6 (April, 1925), pp. 267-9.

      Discusses the term "modern" as characterized by the
      "chaotic in the metaphysical implications of our work,"
      and counts D.H. Lawrence among the modern men of letters.
      The Rainbow is a transitional novel between those that
      obey "the law of yesterday" and the later, more nearly
      modern, novels. This is expressed in Lawrence's style
      as well, which "deteriorates" as a result of "a spiritual
      disintegration," one "similar to that of Joyce, though
      in the Irishman the essentially subjective quality of his
      art renders difficult the observation of his subservience
      to a time trend."

D15   "The Microcosm of New York." Review of Bercovici, Konrad,
      Around the World in New York. *The Nation* 120, 3118
      (April 8, 1925), p. 388.

D16   "Sicilian Tragedies." Review of Verga, Giovanni, *Little
      Novels of Sicily*. *New York Herald Tribune Books*
      (April 19, 1925), p. 14.

D17   "A Negative Zarathustra." Review of Unamuno, Miguel de,
      Essays and Soliloquies. *New York Herald Tribune Books*
      (May 3, 1925), pp. 2-3.

D18   "A Relic." Review of Manuel, Don Juan, *Count Lucanor,
      Or the Fifty Pleasant Tales of Patronio*. *New York
      Herald Tribune Books* (May 10, 1925), p. 11.

D19   "Benavente as a Dramatist." Review of Starkie, Walter,
      Jacinto Benavente. *New York Herald Tribune Books*
      (June 7, 1925), p. 10.

D20 "A Literary Magnate." Review of Blasco Ibañez, Vicente, *The Old Woman of the Movies and Other Stories*. *New York Herald Tribune Books* (June 21, 1925), p. 9.

D21 Review of Miró, Gabriel, *Figures of the Passion of Our Lord*. *The Nation* 121, 3133 (July 22, 1925), p. 123.

D22 "Miguel de Unamuno." Review of Unamuno, Miguel de, *Essays and Soliloquies*. *The Nation* 121, 3142 (September 23, 1925), pp. 336-7.

D23 "Heirlooms." Review of Peers, E. Allison, *Spanish Mysticism*. *New York Herald Tribune Books* (November 8, 1925), p. 11.

D24 Review of Blasco Ibañez, Vicente, *Alfonso XIII Unmasked*. *New York Herald Tribune Books* (1925? Information unverifiable).

D25 "Son of Ulysses." Review of Shipley, Joseph T., *King John*. *New York Herald Tribune Books* (January 10, 1926), p. 15.

D26 "Entertaining Persiflage." Review of Madariaga, Salvador de, ed., *The Sacred Giraffe*. *The Nation* 123, 3186 (July 28, 1926), p. 89.

D27 "From the Portuguese?" Review of Queiroz, Eça de, *The Relic*. *New York Herald Tribune Books* (October 11, 1926), p. 13.

D28 "A New Look at Cervantes." Review of Castro, Américo, *El Pensamiento de Cervantes*. *The Nation* 123, 3203 (November 23, 1926), pp. 535-6.

D29 "Toward a Revaluation." Review of Ryner, Han, *The Ingenious Hidalgo Miguel Cervantes*. *The Nation* 125, 3235 (July 6, 1927), pp. 20-1.

D30 "A Philosophy of Renunciation." Review of Santayana, George, *Platonism and the Spiritual Life*. *The Nation* 125, 3247 (September 28, 1927), p. 316.

D31 "Transcendental Romanticism." Review of Unamuno, Miguel de, *The Life of Don Quixote and Sancho, According to Miguel Cervantes de Saavedra*. *The Nation* 125, 3255 (November 23, 1927), p. 578.

D31a   "Unamuno's Quixote." Review of Unamuno, Miguel de,
       The Life of Don Quixote and Sancho, According to
       Miguel Cervantes de Saavedra. *New York Herald*
       Tribune Books (December 4, 1927), pp. 18, 20.

       Reprint of D31.

D32   "Historian of Our Stupidity." Review of Mencken, H.L.,
       Prejudices, Sixth Series, and *Selected Prejudices*. *The*
       Nation 126, 3270 (March 7, 1928), pp. 272-3.

D33   "Santayana's Roots." Review of Santayana, George, *The*
       Realm of Essence, Book First of Realms of Being. *The*
       Nation 126, 3275 (April 11, 1928), pp. 410-1.

       Analyzes Santayana's work as the expression of a deep
       need to find "liberation and detachment" through his
       system of philosophy, but faults the work as being a
       retreat from reality and "the contingent"--a form of
       "moral" and "realistic" suicide.

D34   "John Dewey's Humanism." Review of Ratner, Joseph, ed.,
       The Philosophy of John Dewey. *The Nation* 127, 3304
       (October 31, 1928), pp. 457-8.

D35   "A Modern Poet." Review of Leonard, William Ellery, *A*
       Son of Earth. *The Nation* 127, 3309 (December 5,
       1928), p. 624.

D36   Review of Oaks, Gladys, *Nursery Rhymes for Children of*
       Darkness. *The Wisconsin Literary Magazine* 28, 2
       (February, 1929), pp. 27-8.

D37   "Intellectualism in Vacuo." Review of McKeon, Richard,
       The Philosophy of Spinoza, and Wolf, A., ed., *The*
       Correspondence of Spinoza. *The Nation* 128, 3320
       (February 20, 1929), pp. 228-9.

D38   "Southern Prophet." Review of Rodó, José E., *The Motives*
       of Proteus. *The Nation* 128, 3327 (April 10, 1929),
       pp. 429-30.

D39   "Popular Morals." Review of Ayers, C.E., *Holier Than*
       Thou: The Way of the Righteous. *The Nation* 119,
       3347 (August 29, 1929), pp. 228-9.

D40   "Rabelais." Review of Nock, Albert J., and Wilson, C.R.,
       François Rabelais: The Man and His Work, and Putnam,
       Samuel, *François Rabelais: Man of the Renaissance*. *The*
       Nation 130, 3373 (February 26, 1930), pp. 250-2.

D41 Review of Krutch, Joseph Wood, *Experience & Art*. *The Wisconsin State Journal* 141, 64 (December 4, 1932), p. 3.

D42 "One More Christian." Review of Mackay, John A., *The Other Spanish Christ*. *The Nation* 136, 3532 (March 15, 1933), p. 293.

D43 "Guedalla Facing South." Review of Guedalla, Philip, *Argentine Tango*. *The Nation* 136, 3535 (April 5, 1933), p. 380.

D44 "Francis Bacon." Review of Williams, Charles, *Bacon*. *The Nation* 138, 3587 (April 4, 1934), p. 393.

D45 "About Modern Poetry." Review of Sparrow, John, *Sense and Poetry*. *The Wisconsin State Journal* 144, 8 (April 8, 1934), p. 4.

D46 "Critic of American Culture." Review of Brooks, Van Wyck, *Three Essays on America*. *The Wisconsin State Journal* 144, 57 (May 27, 1934), p. 4.

D47 "Baruch or Benedictus." Review of Wolfson, Harry A., *The Philosophy of Spinoza*, and Melamed, S.M., *Spinoza and Buddah*. *The Nation* 138, 3607 (August 22, 1934), pp. 222–4.

D48 "Ezra Pound." Review of Pound, Ezra, *ABC of Reading*. *The Wisconsin State Journal* 145, 21 (October 21, 1934), p. 4.

D49 "Jean-Jacques' Doctrines." Review of Hendel, Charles W., *Jean-Jacques Rousseau, Moralist*. *The Nation* 139, 3611 (September 19, 1934), pp. 334–5.

D50 "Max Eastman." Review of Eastman, Max, *Art and the Life of Action*. *The Wisconsin State Journal* 145, 42 (November 11, 1934), p. 7.

D51 Review of Krutch, Joseph Wood, *Was Europe a Success?* *The Capital Times* 35, 86 (March 10, 1935), p. 22.

D52 Review of Rothschild, Edward F., *The Meanings of Unintelligibility in Modern Art*. *The Wisconsin State Journal* (April, 1935).

D53 "A Liberal Historian." Review of Becker, Carl L.,
       Everyman His Own Historian. *The Nation* 140, 3642
       (April 24, 1935), pp. 487-8.

D54 "Analysis of Renoir's Art." Review of Barnes, Albert C.,
       and Mazia, Violette de, *The Art of Renoir*. *The Nation*
       141, 3660 (August 28, 1935), p. 250.

D55 "Mr. Santayana's Wisdom." Review of Santayana, George,
       Obiter Scripta. *The Nation* 142, 3694 (April 22,
       1936), pp. 524-5.

D56 "Buck Looks Back." Review of Buck, Philo M., *The
       World's Great Age*. *The Wisconsin State Journal* 148,
       40 (May 10, 1936), p. 4.

D57 "Mr. Prall's Aesthetics." Review of Prall, D.W., *Aesthetic
       Analysis*. *The Nation* 142, 3701 (June 10, 1936), p. 752.

       Notes the confusion in Prall's usage between "feeling"
       and "emotion." Denies that art expresses emotion. "It
       arouses emotion, but it is in inverse proportion to the
       degree of rapt attention we pay it." Notes also some
       confusion in Prall's notion of "aesthetic" apprehension.

D58 Review of Linton, Ralph, *The Study of Man*. *The Capital
       Times* 38, 99 (September 27, 1936), p. 22.

       D58a "A Proper Study." Review of Linton, Ralph,
              The Study of Man. *The Nation* 143, 22 (November
              28, 1936), p. 639.

              Reprint of D58.

D59 "Mr. Santayana's Philosophy." Review of Edman, Irwin,
       ed., *The Philosophy of Santayana*. *The Nation* 143, 17
       (October 24, 1936), pp. 495-6.

D60 Review of Knox, Israel, *The Aesthetic Theories of Kant,
       Hegel and Schopenhauer*. *The Nation* 144, 7 (February 13,
       1937), p. 192.

D61 "Bankrupt Realism." Review of Pratt, James B., *Personal
       Realism*. *The Nation* 144, 11 (March 13, 1937), pp.
       300-1.

D62 "The Philosophy of Aldous Huxley." Review of Huxley,
       Aldous, *Eyeless in Gaza*. *Marxist Quarterly* 1, 2
       (April-June 1937), pp. 315-9.

D63 "Anti-Metaphysical Philosophy." Review of Carnap, Rudolph, *The Logical Syntax of Language*, and Weinberg, Julius, *An Examination of Logical Positivism*. *The Nation* 144, 21 (May 22, 1937), pp. 599-600.

D64 "Our Nietzsche." Review of *The Philosophy of Nietzsche* (Modern Library Edition). *The Nation* 144, 25 (June 19, 1937), pp. 710-1.

D65 "Professor Hartshorne's God." Review of Hartshorne, Charles, *Beyond Humanism*. *The Nation* 145, 1 (July 3, 1937), p. 24.

Criticizes Hartshorne's attempt to establish "belief in the God of the 'new' science and the 'new' theology."

D66 "Mussolini's Philosopher." Review of Holmes, Roger W., *The Idealism of Giovanni Gentile*. *The Nation* 145, 16 (October 16, 1937), pp. 410-1.

D67 "Toward an Improved Strategy." Review of Burke, Kenneth, *Attitudes Toward History*. *The Nation* 145, 26 (December 25, 1937), p. 723.

D68 "Types of Philosophy." Review of Edman, Irwin, *Four Ways of Philosophy*. *The New Republic* 93, 1205 (January 5, 1938), p. 262.

D69 "The Problems of Morals." Review of Stace, W.T., *The Concept of Morals*. *The Nation* 146, 3 (January 15, 1938), p. 76.

Attacks Stace's "half-hearted empiricism" for failing to confront the problem of "practical adjustment": a thorough-going reconstruction of human institutions."

D70 "The Error of Philosophy." Review of Gilson, Etienne, *The Unity of Philosophical Experience*. *The Nation* 146, 8 (February 19, 1938), pp. 219-20.

D71 "Beauty as Quality." Review of Pepper, Stephen C., *Aesthetic Quality*. *The Nation* 146, 17 (April 23, 1938), pp. 481-2.

Praises Pepper's book as "foundational for practical criticism," though it faults the book for "defining emotion as the 'essence of quality.'" Remarks, in the end, that Pepper's version of pragmatism is self-styled "contextualism."

D72 "A Conservative Testifies." Review of Vilaplana, Ruiz,
       Burgos Justice. *The New Republic* 94, 1221 (April 27,
       1938), p. 366.

D73 "The Dialectic According to Levy." Review of Levy, H.,
       A Philosophy for Modern Man. *Partisan Review* 4, 6
       (May, 1938), pp. 51-4.

D74 "Logic and the Scientific Method." Review of Dewey,
       John, *Logic, the Theory of Inquiry*. *The Saturday
       Review* 19, 2 (November 5, 1938), p. 18.

D75 "Art as Expression." Review of Collingwood, R.G., *The
       Principles of Art*. *The Nation* 148, 4 (January 21,
       1939), pp. 98-9.

       Reflects his appreciation of Collingwood's aesthetics--
       of considerable influence (along with Dewey, Croce, and
       Cassirer) in forming the "idealistic" dimension of Vivas'
       position.

D76 "Hyperindividualism." Review of Weiss, Paul, *Reality*.
       The Nation 149, 2 (July 8, 1939), pp. 50-1.

D77 "Introduction to Dewey." Review of Hook, Sidney, *John
       Dewey*. *The Nation* 150, 1 (January 6, 1940), pp. 22-3.

D78 "Too Wild a Cow for Our Matador." Review of Tindall,
       William York, *D.H. Lawrence and Susan His Cow*. *Partisan
       Review* 7, 1 (January-February, 1940), pp. 67-9.

       States flatly that Tindall lacks the "qualifications"
       to write a definitive study of Lawrence, first because
       he "hates his subject" and second because he "lacks an
       adequate sense of his problem."

D79 Review of Wolf, A., *A History of Science, Technology and
       Philosophy in the Eighteenth Century*. *The Nation* 150,
       12 (March 23, 1940), pp. 401-2.

D80 "Critique of Santayana." Review of Munitz, Milton K.,
       The Moral Philosophy of George Santayana. *The Nation*
       151, 2 (July 13, 1940), p. 37.

D81 "The Philosophy of Peirce." Review of Buchler, Justus,
       Charles Peirce's Empiricism. *The Nation* 151, 20
       (November 16, 1940), pp. 483-4.

D82 "Positive Ethics." Review of Schlick, Moritz, *Problems of Ethics*. *The Kenyon Review* 2, 1 (Winter, 1940), pp. 109-12.

D83 "Mr. Russell on Empiricism." Review of Russell, Bertrand, *An Enquiry into Meaning and Truth*. *The Nation* 152, 10 (March 8, 1941), pp. 275-6.

D84 Review of Buck, Philo M., *Directions in Contemporary Literature*. *Daily Cardinal* 51, 138 (April 4, 1942), p. 4.

D85 "From Prometheus to Maitreya." Review of Morris, Charles, *Paths of Life*. *The Kenyon Review* 4, 3 (Autumn, 1942), pp. 419-22.

D86 Review of Brinton, Crane, *Nietzsche*, and Morgan, George Allen, *What Nietzsche Means*. *American Sociological Review* 7, 6 (December, 1942), pp. 883-6.

D87 Review of Muller, Herbert J., *Science & Criticism*. *Accent* 4, 1 (Autumn, 1943), pp. 58-60.

D88 "M. Maritain's Aesthetics." Review of Maritain, Jacques, *Art and Poetry*. *The Nation* 158, 17 (April 22, 1944), pp. 488-9.

Resists Maritain's "dogmatism" while at the same time acknowledging the contribution of Maritain's aesthetics--especially his insistence upon the truly creative dimension of art.

D89 "A Forerunner of Existentialism." Review of Kierkegaard, Søren, *Works of Love*. *Chicago Sun Book Week* (August 11, 1946).

Explains the elements of Kierkegaard to a general audience in terms that reveal appreciation for the Dane's "value"--"he challenges all the facile assumptions and presuppositions of modern life by defining human destiny in stern, uncompromising, religious terms and by repudiating radically the secularism of the modern world."

D90 "Franz Kafka's Fine Writings." Review of Flores, Angel, ed., *The Kafka Problem*, and *A Franz Kafka Miscellany*, Prombaum, Sophie, and Humphreys-Roberts, G., trans. *Chicago Sun Book Week* (November 3, 1946), p. 9.

Expresses appreciation of Flores' collection as throwing "a good deal of light on what Kafka was about," to

wit, presenting in his poems a "peculiarly dualistic or
dialectical conception of the world." Of particular
interest in Kafka's world is that Kafka sees man "as
caught in a net of relationships, which, as one seeks to
explore them, reveal themselves as tauntingly but elusive-
ly rational in their essence but at the same time as some-
how no less essentially mysterious and absurd."

D91   Review of Schilpp, Paul, ed., *The Philosophy of Ernst
      Cassirer. The Journal of Aesthetics and Art Criticism*
      8, 3 (January, 1950), pp. 275-6.

      Praises Cassirer's work and regrets that it is not more
      widely known among critics who might then cease their
      "perfectly sterile discussion ... as to the capacity of
      art to give us positive knowledge."

D92   "Lorca's Background." Review of Barea, Arturo, *Lorca,
      the Poet and His People. Poetry* 76, 1 (April, 1950),
      pp. 46-51.

D93   "Our Spiritual Heritage." Review of Highet, Gilbert,
      *The Classical Tradition. Greek and Roman Influences on
      Western Literature. The Western Review* 15, 2 (Winter,
      1951), pp. 152-4.

      Praises the book but faults Highet for ignoring the
      gradual deterioration of Western civilization out of a
      preoccupation with "catastrophe."

D94   Review of Henle, Paul, et al., eds., *Structure, Method,
      and Meaning. Essays in Honor of Henry M. Scheffer.
      The Journal of Aesthetics and Art Criticism* 10, 3
      (March, 1952), pp. 279-80.

      Focuses on the Langer essay and the question of whether
      her notion of "significant form" is an advance over the
      Bell-Fry theory that the significance of form lies in
      the emotion it arouses.

D95   Review of Boas, George, *Wingless Pegasus*, and Weitz,
      Morris, *Philosophy of the Arts. Ethics* 62, 3 (April,
      1952), pp. 222-4.

      Criticizes Boas' interest theory of value that would
      reduce ethics to psychology. Notes with approval Weitz's
      claim that the reduction of value to preference is
      nihilistic and as such "totally unacceptable to the
      demands of human experience." (This theme is taken up
      by Vivas in Part I of *The Moral Life and the Ethical
      Life*, A1.)

D96   "Evolutionary Aesthetics and Aristotle." Review of
       Jenkins, Iredell, *Art and the Human Enterprise*, and
       Else, Gerald F., *Artistotle's Poetics: The Argument*.
       The Yale Review 48, 1 (September, 1958), pp. 135-9.

       Discusses Jenkins' attempt to blend "what is best in
       the theory of expression with what he takes to be the
       irrefragable truth of imitation." Taking music as a
       point of focus, Vivas asks whether it is not more ac-
       curate to say that music "in-forms emotions than to say
       [it] *symbolizes* emotion."

D97   "For and Against the Founder." Review of Hook, Sidney,
       ed., *Psychoanalysis, Scientific Method and Philosophy*.
       National Review 7, 26 (October 10, 1959), pp. 398-400.

       Asks whether the collection of essays "contributes to
       our *knowledge* of man," and discusses the narrow, positiv-
       istic criterion of acceptability that questions the
       legitimacy of Freudian "philosophy."

D98   Review of Weiss, Paul, *Our Public Life*. *Ethics* 70, 2
       (January, 1960), pp. 168-71.

       Speaks highly of Weiss's book--especially its attempt
       "to rejoin what modern philosophy long ago sundered:
       fact and value," and for providing a naturalistic phi-
       losophy that is less objectionable than most. Questions
       Weiss's characterization of man as one "who prospers be-
       cause he is afraid" and the possibility of generating a
       concept of "right" from a naturalistic account of human
       nature.

D99   "A Theory of Man." Review of Harris, Marjorie S.,
       Francisco Romero on Problems of Philosophy. *The
       Randolph-Macon Alumnae Bulletin* 54, 1 (November, 1960),
       pp. 4-6.

D100   "Something for Everybody." Review of Burnshaw, Stanley,
       ed., *Varieties of Literary Experience*. *The Sewanee
       Review* 71, 2 (Spring, 1963), pp. 343-7.

       Provides an overview of the book's contents and ex-
       presses regret that, typically, Cleanth Brooks's essay
       reveals an absence of theoretical depth.

D101   "Essays After a 180 Degree Turn in Thought." Review of
       Dos Passos, John, *Occasions and Protest*. *Chicago
       Tribune Books Today* (December 20, 1964), p. 3.

D102   "Something Is Missing." Review of Frankel, Charles,
       The Love of Anxiety and Other Essays. *New York Times
       Book Review* (July 18, 1965), pp. 6-7.

D103   "Incoherent Nihilist." Review of Marcuse, Herbert,
       Five Lectures, Psychoanalysis, Politics, and Utopia.
       National Review 22, 27 (July 14, 1970), pp. 739-42.

D104   "Ordeal of Civilization." Review of Luckas, John, *The
       Passing of the Modern Age*. *National Review* 22, 40
       (October 20, 1970), pp. 1116-7.

D105   "Too Clever By Half." Review of Steiner, George, *In
       Bluebeard's Castle: Some Notes Toward the Redefinition
       of Culture*. *National Review* 23, 51 (December 31,
       1971), pp. 1477-8.

D106   Review of Spector, Jack J., *The Aesthetics of Freud:
       A Study in Psychoanalysis and Art*. *Leonardo* 8, 1
       (Winter, 1975).

       Criticizes Freud's tendency to dismiss art as an ex-
       pression of neurosis and questions Freud's account of
       creativity and lack of concern for the object of art--
       as opposed to its maker.

E

LECTURES AND SPEECHES

E1   "The Futility of Social Science." Hillel Foundation
      Lecture, October 31, 1930.

E2   "The Good Life for Modern Man." Unity Forum at Madison,
      Wisconsin, March, 1938.

E3   "Criticism, Intrinsic and Extrinsic." Mahlon Powell
      Lecture at Indiana University, July 22, 1952 (see C74).

E4   "Aesthetics and the Theory of Signs." Mahlon Powell
      Lecture at Indiana University, July 24, 1952 (see C75).

E5   "The Function of Literature: Two Views and a Third." The
      Nineteenth Peter Rushton Seminar in Contemporary Prose
      and Poetry at the University of Virginia, March 25, 1960.

E6   "Literature and Ideology." Alumni Fund Lecture at North-
      western University, April 27, 1960 (see C95).

E7   "The Need for a Conservative Philosophy." Conference
      organized by the Foundation for Economic Education,
      May 17, 1965.

E8   "The Universities Then and Now." Philadelphia Society,
      Chicago, 1967.

E9   "The Educated Man." Honors Convocation at Rockford
      College, May 1, 1971.

E10   "On Hofstader's 'Art and Knowledge.'" American Society
      for Aesthetics, Fall, 1971.

E11   "On Moral Philosophy." Hillsdale College, 1972.

Part II
Secondary Sources

BOOKS AND COLLECTIONS OF ESSAYS

F1 Curtler, Hugh Mercer. *A Theory of Art, Tragedy and Litera-
    ture: The Philosophy of Eliseo Vivas.* New York: Haven
    Publishing Corp., 1981.

   Contents: Part One: Vivas, Poetic Philosopher; Part Two:
   Moral and Ethical Values (Argument from Adequacy: Epistemic
   Objectivity, Values and the Moral Life, Moral Justification,
   Reconciliation and the Epilogue to *Crime and Punishment*,
   Persons, Problems with Axiological Realism); Part Three:
   The Philosophy of Art (Creation and Discovery, Transaction
   and Symbolism, Values and Their Requiredness: Some Examples,
   Literary Criticism, Some Objections to Vivas' Aesthetics);
   Part Four: Vivas' Philosophy of Culture (Tragedy, Cultural
   Relativism, Naturalism and Scientism, Contra Marcuse);
   Part Five: Overview of Vivas' System.

   Examines Vivas' major writings to show the systematic
   underpinnings that hold them together. Begins with an
   examination of Vivas' axiological realism and then shows
   how his aesthetics and critical theory rest comfortably on
   that foundation. Addresses the presumed inconsistency
   between Vivas' phenomenalism and his realism (see introduction to this bibliography and cf. Lee Brown, G6) and
   argues that Vivas is a realistic phenomenologist--as was
   Nicolai Hartmann from whom Vivas borrowed leading ideas.
   Contends that Vivas' tragic vision forms a bridge between
   his aesthetics and his philosophy of culture and that his
   conservatism was born out of his realism.

F2 Regnery, Henry, ed. *¡Viva Vivas!* Indianapolis: Liberty
    Press, 1976. 379 pp.

   A Festschrift, in honor of Vivas' 75th birthday, containing eleven essays and a bibliography of Vivas' published
   works. Essays cover all of Vivas' work minus his work in
   ethics (except as it bears on "the political life"). Included are tributes from William Earle and the editor,

exposition of Vivas' aesthetics by Murray Krieger and
Peter Stanlis, and a critical examination of the concept
of "intransitive attention" by Lee Brown. Several essays
have nothing to do with Vivas, though Kenner's essay sheds
important light on the problem Brown (and others) discusses
(see G38).

Specifically, the book contains the following essays:
1. "For and About Eliseo Vivas," by Henry Regnery. 2.
"Styled Thought: An Open Letter to Eliseo Vivas," by
William Earle (G13). 3. "The Theoretical Contributions
of Eliseo Vivas," by Murray Krieger (G24). 4. "The Ethical
Life and the Political Life," by David Levy (G27). 5.
"The Sacred and Golden Cord," by William T. Couch. 6.
"The Aesthetic Theory of Eliseo Vivas," by Peter J. Stanlis
(G37). 7. "Animadversions on the Autonomy of Art," by Lee
B. Brown (G6). 8. "Vivas, Lawrence, Eliot, and the Demon,"
by Russell Kirk (G23). 9. "Eliseo Vivas: Philosopher in
Spite of Himself," by Stephen J. Tonsor (G41). 10. "Arthur
Schopenhauer," by Erich Heller. 11. "The Study of Asian
Philosophy: For History, for Comparison, for Synthesis?"
by Robert Browning.

ESSAYS AND REVIEW ARTICLES

G1 Aiken, Henry D. "Aesthetics on the Stretch." Review of
    Creation and Discovery (A2). *Kenyon Review* 18 (1955),
    pp. 633-9.

    Examines Vivas' book in light of his break with natural-
    ism and comments on the theoretical strain produced by his
    realism bedded down with his older naturalistic tendencies--
    both of which Aiken finds present in this collection of
    essays. Concludes that "he has still not succeeded in
    showing how a work of art can be aesthetically pure in
    his sense, and yet also be a porch from which we may view
    realms of being to which the more discursive understanding
    has no access."
    Contends that Vivas' acceptance of axiological realism
    to shore up his aesthetics is due to a misunderstanding of
    the way language functions: "the thesis that the only
    fundamental use of words is to tell what there is." Addi-
    tionally, Aiken faults Vivas for his doctrine of "intransi-
    tive attention" as "all but useless ... for anyone serious-
    ly interested in understanding what happens when we read
    poetry or look at a picture."

G2 Bertocci, Angelo. "Eliseo Vivas' Aesthetics Since the
    Artistic Transaction" (unpublished).

    Contains a lengthy exposition of Vivas' latest work in
    aesthetics which the author states he wrote for himself
    "to get clear what the problems are for me in an aesthetics
    that has intrigued and puzzled me for the last ten years
    or more...."

G3 ————. Review of *D.H. Lawrence: The Failure and Triumph
    of Art* (A3). *Comparative Literature* 14, 2 (Spring,
    1962), pp. 208-15.

    Argues that Vivas provides in this book a test of his
    theory of "organismic" criticism, a theory that involves

a "rigid adherence to aesthetic rigorism." What is new
"and of major interest in this book is the conscious and
consistent application of a contextualist criticism to
the bulk of the work of D.H. Lawrence." Expresses difficulties (as does Heilman, G19) with Vivas' notion of how
"dreadful" or "obscene" subject matter can interfere with
an aesthetic grasp of a poem. Suggests that it is "the
moral man Vivas who has refused *après coup*, to apprehend
such an object [as "The Woman Who Rode Away"] aesthetically." (On this point, see Vivas, *The Artistic Transaction*
(A4), pp. 42 ff.)

Contrasts Vivas' treatment of Lawrence with that of F.R.
Leavis and prefers Vivas' criticism as being "critical
first of itself."

G4 ————. Review of *The Artistic Transaction and Essays in
   the Theory of Literature* (A4). *Comparative Literature*
   17, 2 (Spring, 1965), pp. 173-7.

Provides a lengthy exposition of the book under review
with the lead essay in sharp focus. Raises several questions that Vivas comments on in his essay "Reply to Some
Criticisms" (C109) among which is included an especially
probing question: "in the face of conflict of intuitions
or immanent meanings, who shall be arbiter and on the
basis of what criteria?"

G5 Brennan, Joseph. "The Role of Emotion in Aesthetic Experience." *Quarterly Journal of Speech* 40 (December,
   1954), pp. 422-8.

Attacks the view that art is simply an affair of reliev-
ing feelings though not to the point of accepting Vivas'
notion of the pure aesthetic experience. Claims that such
a view (as Vivas') is "puritanical--as if there were something about emotion which was not quite nice." Accepts
Vivas' distinction between emotion and feeling and discusses briefly the "cognitive aspects of feeling as opposed
to the sympathetic character of emotion."

G6 Brown, Lee B. "Animadversions on the Autonomy of Art."
   ¡*Viva Vivas!* (F2), pp. 183-224.

Echoes the criticism of Walter Sutton (G38 and G39) and
others that attention to a work of literature cannot ex-
clude reference outside the work itself in the form of
"philosophically pointed visions." Indeed, "no aesthetic
perception is free from these conceptual factors."

Contends that there is some inconsistency between the realistic and the idealistic tenets of Vivas' thought which is, nonetheless, "thoroughly systematic."

G7   Brown, Merle. "Vivas and Croce." *Revista di Studi
      Crociani* 5 (July-September, 1968), pp. 304-8.

Points out similarities between Croce and Vivas who is his "semblable" and also "one of the most influential philosophers in America." Notes that Vivas is writing within "a much weaker critical tradition [than did Croce], a tradition which may in fact lack even one great critic," and that Vivas' aesthetics is stronger than his criticism. Regrets, in the end, that Vivas has not carried over his theory of the moral personality into aesthetics and that he failed to distinguish between art and entertainment. Concludes with high praise of Vivas "despite his weak sense of history."

G8   ———. "The Philosopher Critic." Scholes, R., ed.,
      The Philosopher Critic. Tulsa: University of Tulsa
      Press, 1970, pp. 3-12.

Examines the differences between philosophy and criticism in the light of the "ideal" philosopher/critic exemplified by Benedetto Croce and Eliseo Vivas. Faults both Croce and Vivas for failing to distinguish between critical judgment and critical interpretation. The latter is almost totally ignored by both thinkers and is more nearly poetry than philosophy. Argues that increased attention to interpretation, or "characterization," would mitigate the radical distinction between poetic and philosophical modes of knowing peculiar to both thinkers.

G9   Curtler, Hugh Mercer. "Eliseo Vivas on Value." *Modern
      Age* 22, 1 (Winter, 1978), pp. 18-27.

Summarizes Vivas' axiological realism and his criticism of cultural relativism. Shows how Vivas' conservatism arises out of his realism in light of his sense of human tragedy. Contains portions of several chapters of the book-length study of Vivas' philosophy, *A Theory of Art, Literature and Tragedy: The Philosophy of Eliseo Vivas* (F1).

G10   ———. "Vivas and Camus on Tragedy." *Centennial Review*
      23, 1 (Winter, 1979), pp. 79-90.

Exhibits some of the parallels between the views of Vivas and Albert Camus on tragedy. Contains a close examination of Vivas' notion of "unmitigated tragedy" (C114

and C119) in light of his aesthetic theory and insofar
as it provides a perspective on Vivas' philosophy of
culture.

G11 Dickie, George. "The Myth of the Aesthetic Attitude."
     American Philosophical Quarterly 1, 1 (January, 1964),
     pp. 56-65.

     Contends, *contra* Vivas, Jerome Stolnitz, et al., that
     the "aesthetic attitude" is simply a matter of paying
     attention to a work of art--no more and no less. Denies
     the possibility of imaginative/affective response devoid
     of cognition (see Brown, G6, and Sutton, G38 and G39) and
     tends to ignore the question of the object of the aesthetic
     attitude. On this last point, see the introduction to
     this bibliography.

G12 ———. "I.A. Richards' Phantom Double." *The British
     Journal of Aesthetics* 8 (January, 1968), pp. 54-9.

     Expresses general agreement with Vivas' confusion over
     Richards' notion of the "balance of opposed impulses" in
     the aesthetic experience and develops his own criticisms
     of the view along the lines of Vivas and Max Black.

G13 Earle, William. "Styled Thought: An Open Letter to
     Eliseo Vivas." *¡Viva Vivas!* (F2), pp. 23-36.

     Pays tribute to Eliseo Vivas whose "thought bears upon
     the universal, but [whose] manner of expression is per-
     sonal and poetic." Contends that the passions of the man,
     his "capacity for mockery, piety, courtesy, anger, love
     and outrage" all "pass into his thought, strict, informed,
     and courageous unto belligerency."

G14 Edel, Abraham. "Vivas and the Dragons of Naturalism."
     Review of Metaphysics 5, 3 (March, 1952), pp. 436-42.

     Reviews, at some length, Vivas' *The Moral Life and the
     Ethical Life* (A1) and dwells on Vivas' rejection of
     naturalism and the realism he would offer in its place.
     Focuses on Vivas' notion of the person and compains that
     this notion is really no improvement over the naturalistic,
     value-free alternatives. "Vivas' use of 'the espoused
     values of the other as person' to keep the moral process
     open is no different in specific moral effect from Dewey's
     recognition that claims arise naturally in all social
     relationships...." Insists that Vivas "has not altogether
     emancipated himself from [the failings] of contemporary
     naturalism" and that he could do so only by bringing in

the "religious values and beliefs his view suggests at
the beginning."
    Counters Vivas' attacks against cultural relativism
and evidences little patience with Vivas' axiological
realism which he finds "simply adds to the confusion of
the contemporary crisis."

G15 Foster, Richard. *The New Romantics: A Reappraisal of the
     New Criticism*. Bloomington: Indiana University Press,
     1962, pp. 64-81.

    Traces Vivas' abandonment of "neo-positivism" for
"romantic humanism" as evidenced by the rhetoric employed
in key essays written during the 1940's and 1950's. Notes
the "ferocity" of Vivas' anti-positivistic reaction and
the birth of his "sentimental jargon of certain belle-
tristic concepts that we are likely to associate with the
aesthetic thought of the earlier nineteenth century."
The result is a relaxing of method that results in "some
philosophical weaknesses" if not abandonment of philosophy
altogether for the "more humanistically limber role of
critic and man of letters."

G16 Hausman, Carl R. "Some Questions Concerning Eliseo Vivas'
     The Moral Life and The Ethical Life." (unpublished.)

    Begins with an account of Vivas' book and then raises
three problems with the thesis contained therein: (1) What
is the relation of man's "telic aspect" to the ground of
moral authority? (2) Is it not possible to attain "in-
corrigible intuitions"? If not, how does one ground his
epistemology? (3) Does a concern for the primacy of persons necessarily entail pacifism?

G17 ————. "Mechanism and Teleology in the Creative Process."
     Journal of Philosophy 58 (Spring, 1961), pp. 577-83.

    Explains the paradox elaborated later (G18) by seeking
an account of the creative process "which accounts for
the production of something new in respect to the conditions existing prior to creation." Defends Vivas' "teleo-
logical view" of creation ("Naturalism and Creativity,"
C54a) as against Vincent Thomas' mechanistic attack on
that view (see G40).

G18 ————. Review of *The Artistic Transaction and Essays on
     Theory of Literature* (A4). *International Philosophical
     Quarterly* 4, 2 (May, 1964), pp. 297-316.

    Summarizes Vivas' book briefly and then criticizes the
views he finds there. Faults Vivas for failing to provide

a defining characteristic of the *aesthetic* mode of
awareness—is it symbolic or is it not? "If the basic
symbolic activity arose after man had been fully engaged
in practical activities, then the aesthetic and the
symbolic responses seem to be undifferentiated qualitatively and to differ only in degree. But if man must
constitute the world in symbols before he can attend to
it purposefully, then the aesthetic and the symbolic may
be qualitatively different." Stresses that "the object
side" of the aesthetic response must be the grounds for
differentiating the aesthetic from the nonaesthetic, lest
Vivas incur the "error of psychologism."

Argues that Vivas needs to distinguish between aesthetic
value and significance on the basis of the claim that
aesthetic value and meaning are a function of the substance
of the work—and not merely its form as suggested in
Vivas' book. Of special concern is the relation of art,
of the meanings and values in a particular work, to
"other modes of experience" and the paradox of how the
new can also be intelligible.

In brief, Hausman shows the need to ground Vivas'
aesthetic in his realism, in the context of a group of
essays that tend to stress the phenomenalistic or idealistic elements of Vivas' thought.

G19   Heilman, Robert B. "Nomad, Monads, and the Mystique of
      the Soma." Review of *D.H. Lawrence: The Failure and
      Triumph of Art* (A3). *The Sewanee Review* (Autumn, 1960),
      pp. 635-59.

Praises Vivas' book as "a very important contribution
to Lawrence criticism" given the "finesse and authority"
of its author, and uses that book as a lever to pry into
the complex relationship between D.H. Lawrence the man
and D.H. Lawrence the poet.

Comments on the attitudes critics have had toward
Lawrence generally, and states his preference for Vivas'
"balanced view," though he doesn't necessarily agree with
everything Vivas has to say. Doubts, for example, that
the measure of art is "the adequacy of the transsubstanc-
ing process," since it tends to make "all successful
dramatic presentations equivalent." Further, Vivas'
notion of the constitutive symbol is "helpful" but tends
to "give primacy to the composition of the scene and
gets away from the composition of the whole."

Argues that Vivas, though an apt "student of texts and
their implication" may be overly concerned to preserve
his notion of intransitive attention. "We need to dis-

tinguish between an incitement to non-aesthetic action which is a violation of intransitivity, and a modification of consciousness which is compatible with it." In this regard, Heilman wonders whether Vivas' concern about "obscenity" in Lawrence's novels is a legitimate aesthetic concern (see Bertocci, G3, and Vivas, C24). Notes that stylistic flaws in Lawrence (which Vivas tends to ignore) frequently interfere with intransitive attention to the poem, and ends by raising the question of the extent of Lawrence's genius.

G20 Hook, Sidney. "A Case Study in Anti-Secularism."
     Review of *The Moral Life and the Ethical Life* (A1).
     Partisan Review 18 (March–April 1951), pp. 232–45.

Presents an outraged reaction to the book under review by way of defending naturalism and expressing confused contempt for axiological realism ("ontic value"). Carries the *ad hominem* argument form to embarassing new depths.

G21 ———. "Philosophy and/or Agony." *Pragmatism and the Tragic Sense of Life*. New York: Basic Books, 1974, pp. 171–83.

Repeats the review cited above, on the whole, as he pillories Vivas for having the gall to abandon naturalism for a view that Hook himself is clearly unable to fathom.

G22 Jenkins, Iredell. "Art and Ontology." *Review of Metaphysics* 9, 4 (June, 1956), pp. 624–35.

Reviews *Creation and Discovery* (A2) with special stress on the ontological status of the work of art. Detects metaphysical elements overlooked by the majority of reviewers. Attempts to exhibit the structure of a "consistent system" to be found in the collection of essays at hand and to elucidate thereby the paradox of creation and discovery. Distinguishes four "distinct levels of being" in Vivas' view of the creative discovery of the artist, through which value is discovered, "insists in" the poem, and then comes to reside in culture. Comprises, with Krieger's essay (G26) and Levy's essay (G27), one of the best expositions of Vivas' aesthetics available in essay form.

G23 Kirk, Russell. "Vivas, Lawrence, Eliot and the Demon."
     ¡Viva Vivas! (F2), pp. 225–50.

Suggests a parallel between Vivas and Eliot with respect to their views of the man D.H. Lawrence, since both found in Lawrence "penetrating insights" alongside "spiritual corruption."

G24   Krieger, Murray. *The New Apologists for Poetry*.
        Minneapolis: University of Minnesota Press, 1956.   225 pp.

        Critically examines several preeminent new critics
        through lenses ground by Krieger's teacher, Eliseo Vivas.
        While the study does not include a section or chapter on
        Vivas himself, it shows his influence at practically every
        turn—as acknowledged by the author in his preface. This
        is true no less of Krieger's argument for the objectivity
        of value than it is of his phenomenology of the creative
        act and his repeated stress on the need for theory in
        criticism.
        Explicates the theoretical framework for "organicism"
        or "contextualism," the terms Krieger and Vivas prefer
        to use in connection with the work of the "new apologists
        for poetry," and which he and Vivas have defended against
        the onslaughts of Walter Sutton. (See Sutton, G38 and
        G39. Also see Vivas' "Contextualism Reconsidered," C81,
        and Murray Krieger's response to Sutton, "Contextualism
        Was Ambitious," *Journal of Aesthetics and Art Criticism*
        21, 1 (Fall, 1962), pp. 81-8.)

G25   ————. *A Window to Criticism*. Princeton: Princeton
        University Press, 1964, pp. 59-63.

        Touches briefly on Vivas' notion of the relation of art
        to culture in his examination of "recent literary theory."
        Provides an analysis of Vivas' view of the difference
        between *subsistence*, *insistence*, and *existence* in his own
        terms, using, as a focal example, Marlowe's *Faustus*.
        (See also Jenkins' essay, G22.)

G26   ————. "The Theoretical Contributions of Eliseo Vivas."
        ¡Viva Vivas! (F2), pp. 37-64.

        Provides, with David Levy's essay (G27) and Iredell
        Jenkins' essay (G22), an accurate and sympathetic view
        of Vivas' aesthetics.

     G26a   ————. "The Theoretical Contributions of Eliseo
              Vivas." *Poetic Presence and Illusion: Essays in
              Critical History and Theory*. Baltimore: Johns
              Hopkins University Press, 1979, pp. 37-63.

              Reprint of G26.

G27   Levy, David. "On Creation and Discovery." *PN Review*
        6, 4 (November, 1964), pp. 31-4.

        Provides a brief but accurate overview of Vivas' aesthet-
        ic theory in the light of his essays in *Creation and Dis-
        covery* (A2). (See also Krieger, G26, and Jenkins, G22.)

G28 ————. "The Ethical Life and the Political Life."
    ¡Viva Vivas! (F2), pp. 65-86.

Argues that "the primacy of the person" is an unmanage-
able notion in political philosophy and that it must give
way to a notion of "the common good." Insists that there
is a "higher requirement than the primacy of the person."

G29 Meikeljohn, Alexander. "Response to Vivas." *The Nation*
    132, 3429 (March 25, 1931), pp. 325-6.

Counters Vivas' argument in his essay "Wisconsin's
Experimental College" (C13) by insisting that Vivas did
not succeed "in providing for his argument a more solid
basis of fact"; that he did not "come into vital contact
with either the principles or the practices which the
college has followed."

G30 Morgan, Douglas. "Creativity Today." *Journal of Aesthet-
    ics and Art Criticism* 12, 1 (September, 1953), pp. 1-24.

Defends a "broadly naturalistic view" of creativity
against the claims of Vivas (and others) that stress the
inadequacy of such a view. Contends that novelty can be
accounted for "within the already familiar categories of
organic emergence." Admittedly, the account "breaks
down," but we can expect "more sensitive and more powerful scientific tools for the heavier tasks ahead," and
these will (presumably) provide us with an adequate,
naturalistic account of creativity at some future time.
Continues on to discuss the creative process and the
personality of the creative artist.

G31 Morris, Wesley. *Toward a New Historicism.* Princeton:
    Princeton University Press, 1972, pp. 177-86.

Examines Vivas' place alongside Leo Spitzer and Charles
Fidelson in the movement toward a "new historicism" that
will correctly assess the place of literature in culture.
The chapter which discusses the three thinkers focuses
upon the "tradition" of new historicism that emphasizes
"the self-sufficiency" and "organic wholeness" of works
of literature. Morris' discussion is largely expository
and lays the groundwork for a more detailed discussion of
the work of Murray Krieger.
    Of special interest is Morris' examination of Vivas'
paradox of creation and discovery in which the author
notes the stress between the metaphysical and phenomenological aspects of Vivas' view: the claims of "value
realism" alongside the exigencies of practical criticism.

In the end, Morris concludes that Vivas' paradox offers
"a stronger sense of the poet's vital rôle in the social
process--a rôle that perhaps ultimately deserves the honor-
ific title of creator.'"

G32   Nemerov, Howard. "Across the Woods and into the Trees."
      Poetry and Fiction: Essays. New Brunswick, N.J.:
      Rutgers University Press, 1963, pp. 319-29.

      Reviews *Creation and Discovery* (A2) in conjunction with
      two other books in a manner that reveals more about Nem-
      erov's distaste for theory and things philosophical than
      it does about Vivas' book.

G33   Santayana, George. "Apologia pro Mente Sua." (Reply to
      Vivas, et al.) *The Philosophy of George Santayana*.
      LaSalle: Open Court Press, 1940, pp. 497-605.

      Acknowledges that Vivas correctly represents his views
      in his paper on *The Life of Reason* and *The Last Puritan*
      (C35) and responds to several of the criticisms while
      ignoring most.

G34   Sellars, Roy Wood. Review of *The Moral Life and the
      Ethical Life* (A1). *Philosophy and Phenomenological
      Research* 12, 3 (March, 1952), pp. 405-16.

      Follows Aiken, Edel, and Hook (G1, G14, and G20 re-
      spectively) in expressing concern over Vivas' abandonment
      of naturalism. Finds Vivas' ideas to be examples of "the
      dramatic, spiritualistic vitalism which is so prominent
      in religio-philosophical circles in France and Germany,
      namely existentialism." [Note that William Earle (G13)
      and Vivas himself, in his preface to the work reviewed,
      admit to strong existentialistic tendencies in Vivas'
      thought.] In the end, Sellars finds the book "for all
      its brilliance ... tangential to the basic currents of
      thought."

G35   Singer, Irving. "Literary Truth." *The Hudson Review* 9
      (Spring, 1956), pp. 141-6.

      Evidences bewilderment at the thought of "such queer
      entities" as values ("ideal objects") that can only be
      discovered by the creative act of poets and artists
      generally. Cannot find any such entities in the works
      of Dreiser, James, Kafka, or Dostoevsky.

G36 Stallknecht, Newton P. Review of *Creation and Discovery* (A2). *Comparative Literature* 8 (1956), pp. 81-5.

Reads the work under review as a work by an author "by disposition a romanticist" who has "undertaken to re-establish the aesthetics of romanticism upon the present scene." (See Foster, G15.) Expresses concern over Vivas' failure to grasp the Aristotelian notion of *mimesis*, while discounting this as a "minor consideration" in light of Vivas' "primary purpose and total contribution."

Provides a generally sympathetic and appreciative grasp of Vivas' paradox of creation and discovery as the "*raison d'être* of the aesthetic life, in a sense, the justification of the humanities."

G37 Stanlis, Peter J. "The Aesthetic Theory of Eliseo Vivas." *iViva Vivas!* (F2), pp. 139-82.

Seeks a grasp of Vivas' aesthetic theory by a reading of the essays in *Creation and Discovery* (A2) and mistaken-ly argues that Vivas "assumes that values have no status in Being independently of men."

G38 Sutton, Walter. "The Contextualist Dilemma--or Fallacy." *Journal of Aesthetics and Art Criticism* 17, 2 (December, 1958), pp. 219-29.

States the following dilemma: that literature can only be grasped contextually but also provides knowledge about the world (it is both referential and nonreferential). Alludes to the attitude of the contextualist critics as an "anti-science" bias which may be viewed as a romantic and symbolist heritage (see Stallknecht, G36, and Foster, G15). Denies that the language of poetry and the language of science differ in important respects and contests Vivas' description of the aesthetic experience. Argues that the "referential functions [of words] are essential to an aesthetic response to the work ... [further, they] determine the aesthetic quality of imaginative literature and control its form." (See also G39 and Vivas' essay "Contextualism Reconsidered," C81, as well as Krieger's essay "Contextualism Was Ambitious," *Journal of Aesthetics and Art Criticism* 21, 1 (Fall, 1962), pp. 81-8. Also see Krieger's book, cited as G24.)

G39 ———. "Contextualist Theory and Criticism as a Social Act." *Journal of Aesthetics and Art Criticism* 19 (Spring, 1961), pp. 317-25.

Defends the view that the "aesthetic response" is not an esoteric experience peculiar to art, but is "an integral

life experience." Contends that contextualism cannot
account for "feelings of revulsion" that often attend
aesthetic experience. Also denies that "rapt, intransitive attention" to a long work of literature is possible
and repeats the claim made in his earlier essay (G38)
that language is primarily referential.

Resists the tendency to dichotomize between the aesthetic
and the nonaesthetic and the claim that the language of
art is different in kind from the language of science.
Insists that contextualism renders criticism impossible
and contests the "intrinsic/extrinsic" distinction in
criticism. (See essays referred to in G38 and also Lee
Brown's essay, G6.)

G40 Tomas, Vincent. "Creativity in Art." *Philosophical
      Review* 67 (January, 1958), pp. 1-15.

Defends the mechanistic view of creativity as against
the views of Vivas in "Naturalism and Creativity" (C54a)
on the grounds that there is no "telic aspect" to creativity (it is not purposive) but is merely controlled by
"critical judgment." (On this point, see Hausman's
essay, G17.)

G41 Tonsor, Stephen J. "Eliseo Vivas: Philosopher in Spite
      of Himself." *¡Viva Vivas!* (F2), pp. 251-72.

Suggests that Vivas mixes poetic intuition, or presentation, with philosophical argument, but that in the end
"Vivas invites us, indeed insists, that we reason about
[truth claims]." Thus, Vivas is a philosopher "in spite
of himself," who nevertheless leaves us with certain
"unresolved problems and difficulties."

G42 Tremmel, William C. "A Footnote to Vivas' Aesthetic
      Transaction." *The Iliff Review* 23, 2 (Spring, 1966),
      pp. 27-31.

Argues that "high religious experience" resembles
aesthetic experience in its intransitivity and should
not therefore be distinguished from aesthetic experience.
Describes this "mystical" experience as one where the
subject/object dichotomy collapses, whereas the spectator
"remains at a distance from the aesthetic object" (cf.
Vivas, C20, and *The Artistic Transaction* (A4), *passim*).

G43 Wheelwright, Philip.   "The Failure of Naturalism (A Reply
         to Eliseo Vivas)."   *The Kenyon Review* 3, 4 (Autumn,
         1941), pp. 460-72.

   Responds to Vivas' "The New Naturalism" (C38) by attack-
ing what Vivas later came to call "scientism," or the view
that the scientific method is the only legitimate method
regardless of the nature of the problem to be solved.
Notes that scientific method is itself subject to "apri-
orism" and is not therefore "methodologically pure."
Defends "intuitive awareness" against the "exactness" of
science, despite its "partial vagueness."   Concludes,
finally, that naturalism cannot "meet men's spiritual
needs" and suggests the idea--later developed by Vivas
himself (*Two Roads to Ignorance* (A6), pp. 164 ff.)--that
scientism rests on a kind of faith (Wheelwright's notion
is that science substitutes "sales talk" for "logic").
In general, the essay anticipates a number of the criticisms that Vivas will level against naturalism later
(see also "A Communication: Reply to Mr. Wheelwright,"
C40).

G44 Wimsatt, William K.   Review of *The Artistic Transaction
         and Essays in the Theory of Literature* (A4).   *Criticism*
         8, 2 (Spring, 1966), pp. 196-202.

   Dwells at length on Vivas' review (C73) of Wimsatt's
own *The Verbal Icon*, by way of a review/response.
   Insists upon the cognitive dimension in the aesthetic
response (see Sutton, G38), and argues that Vivas was
misled into generalizations about "intransitive attention"
to art by his examples which are largely "non-representa-
tional."   Thinks such a view leaves no room for legitimate
criticism, and that "it is time for Mr. Vivas to stop
worrying the aesthetic experience."

H

REVIEWS

H1 *The Moral Life and The Ethical Life* (A1).

    1. Anonymous. *U.S. Quarterly Book Reviews* (March, 1951),
       p. 39.

    2. Barnes, Hazel. *Law Library Book Appraisals* (1963).

    3. Edel, Abraham. *Review of Metaphysics* (March, 1952),
       pp. 436-42. ("Vivas and the Dragons of Naturalism,"
       G14.)

    4. Garnett, A.C. *Christian Century* (Fall, 1951), p. 175.

    5. Hook, Sidney. *Partisan Review* 18 (March-April, 1951),
       pp. 232-45. (G20.)

    6. Kluckhohn, Clyde. *American Anthropologist* (October,
       1951), p. 568.

    7. L., H.A. *Journal of Philosophy* (June, 1951), p. 390.

    8. Nagel, Ernest. *Annals of the Academy of Political
       and Social Science* (May, 1951), p. 208.

    9. Rago, Henry. *Commonweal* (September, 1951), p. 576.

   10. Sellars, Roy Wood. *Philosophy and Phenomenological
       Research* 12, 3 (March, 1952), pp. 405-16.

   11. Spitz, David. *New Republic* 124 (April, 1951), p. 27.

   12. T., M.M. *The Personalist* (Spring, 1952).

   13. Tsanoff, Radoslav A. *New Mexico Quarterly* (Winter,
       1952), pp. 452-7.

   14. Wylleman, A. *Revue Philosophique de Louvain* (1951).

H2 *Creation and Discovery* (A2).

    1. Aiken, Henry D. *The Kenyon Review* 18 (1955), pp. 633-9.
       ("Aesthetics on the Stretch," G1.)

    2. Cahoon, Herbert. *Library Journal* (June, 1955), p. 1500.

    3. Jenkins, Iredell. *Review of Metaphysics* 9 (June,
       1956), pp. 623-37. ("Art and Ontology," G22.)

    4. Martz, Louis M. *The Yale Review* (Autumn, 1955), pp.
       142-6.

    5. Meyer, Frank S. "The Primacy of Art." *The Freeman*
       (December, 1955), p. 796.

    6. Nemerov, Howard. *The Sewanee Review* (October/December,
       1955), p. 655.

   7. Noon, William T., S.J. *Thought*, Vol. 31, pp. 291-3.
   8. Singer, Irving. *Hudson Review* 9 (Spring, 1956),
      pp. 141-6. ("Literary Truth," G35.)
   9. Stallknecht, Newton P. *Comparative Literature* 8
      (1956), pp. 81-5. (G36.)
  10. Zinnes, Harriet. *Poetry* (August, 1956), pp. 339-42.

H3 *D.H. Lawrence: The Failure and Triumph of Art* (A3).

   1. Anonymous. *Nineteenth Century Fiction* (September,
      1960), p. 188.
   2. Anonymous. *Times Literary Supplement* (August, 1961),
      p. 883.
   3. Bacon, W.A. *Christian Century* (November, 1960),
      p. 1380.
   4. Bertocci, Angelo. *Comparative Literature* (Spring,
      1962), pp. 208-15. (G3.)
   5. Chamberlain, John. *The National Review* (August,
      1960), p. 119.
   6. Deasy, Philip. *Commonweal* (Fall, 1961), p. 564.
   7. Harvey, W.J. *Guardian* (August, 1961), p. 6.
   8. Heilman, Robert. *The Sewanee Review* (Autumn, 1960),
      p. 635.
   9. Mayo, Bernard. *Virginia Quarterly* (Autumn, 1960),
      p. 57.
  10. Nyren, Dorothy. *Library Journal* (July, 1960), p. 2595.
  11. Pick, John. *Renaissance* (Spring, 1963), p. 161.
  12. Spilka, Mark. *Modern Philology* (August, 1961), p. 71.
  13. Waggoner, H.H. *The Yale Review* (Autumn, 1960), p. 117.

H4 *The Artistic Transaction and Essays in the Theory of Lit-
    erature* (A4).

   1. Anonymous. *Choice* 1, 1 (March, 1964).
   2. Bertocci, Angelo, *Comparative Literature* (Spring,
      1965), p. 173. (G4.)
   3. Carruth, Hayden. *Poetry* (Spring, 1964), p. 369.
   4. Dickie, George. *Journal of Aesthetics and Art Criti-
      cism* (Spring, 1965), p. 389.
   5. Hausman, Carl R. *International Philosophical Quarterly*
      (May, 1964), pp. 297-316. (G15.)
   6. Tremmel, William C. *Iliff* (Spring, 1966), pp. 27-31.
      (G42.)
   7. Wills, Gary. *The National Review* (June, 1964),
      p. 500.
   8. Wimsatt, William K. *Criticism* (Spring, 1966), p. 196.
      (G44.)

H5   *Contra Marcuse* (A5).

   1. Anonymous. *Kirkus Reviews* (February, 1971), pp. 163-4.
   2. Anonymous. *Publishers Weekly* (January, 1971), p. 53.
   3. Aronson, James. *Antioch Review* (Summer, 1971), p. 288.
   4. Caton, Hiram. *The National Review* (Spring, 1971),
      p. 997.
   5. Kaplan, L.S. *Library Journal* (Fall, 1971), p. 482.
   6. Machan, Tibor. *Journal of Aesthetics and Art Criti-*
      cism (Spring, 1972), p. 40.
   7. Morlino, R.C. *Best Sellers* (July, 1971), p. 166.
   8. Muggeridge, Malcolm. *Esquire* (November, 1971), p. 100.
   9. Rosen, Stanley. *American Political Science Reviewer*
      (December, 1972), p. 1348.
  10. Zoll, Donald A. *Modern Age* (Fall, 1971), p. 425.

H6   *Two Roads to Ignorance* (A6).

   1. Anonymous. *Augusta Chronicle* (April 17, 1980).
   2. Anonymous. *Choice* (March, 1980), p. 269.
   3. Anonymous. *Northwestern Alumni News* (October, 1979).
   4. Bertocci, Angelo. *Iowa Review* (Spring/Summer, 1980), pp.
      284-97.
   5. Brownfield, Allan C. *America's Future* (December 28,
   6. ————. *The Register* (December 31, 1979). Reprint of
      above.
   7. ————. *Human Events* (January 26, 1980), p. 84.
      Reprint of above.
   8. Curtler, Hugh Mercer. *Modern Age* (Spring, 1980),
      pp. 196-8.
   9. Ellmann, Mary. *The Sewanee Review* (Spring, 1980),
      p. 315.
  10. Valdes, Jorge H. *Best Sellers* (February, 1980).

I

DISSERTATIONS

I1 Kraus, Reverend Donald William. "Toward a Realistic
    Theory of Moral Value: A Constructive Study of Perry,
    Vivas and T.V. Smith." Unpublished Doctoral Disserta-
    tion, University of St. Louis, 1959. 213 pp.

Takes Vivas, alongside Ralph Barton Perry and T.V. Smith,
as representative of "widely divergent positions in contemporary value thinking" in order to work toward a "realistic" moral theory along Thomistic lines.
Examines each theory separately, in expository fashion,
and then criticizes each position in order to develop his
own view, stated "in outline fashion," a view that considers value as neither wholly objective nor wholly subjective, but "relational." Value is "the combination of
any tendency and the aptitude (suitability) of the thing
to fulfill it." Grounds value in "the nature of the human
agent" in traditional, Thomistic fashion. This provides
a "schema" of relative worth "in terms of the relative
dignity of the human tendency which they [values] represent."
Provides one of the best accounts in print of Vivas'
moral philosophy and then seeks to "expand his treatment
of the character of value" in the development of a fuller
point of view.
Faults Vivas for the absence of a "self-contained"
axiology, brief and "superficial" phenomenological analyses,
and a "lack of logic," while also noting the "psychological
success" of his attack on naturalism and expressing general
sympathy with Vivas' point of view. Suggests that Vivas
glosses over the differences between aesthetic and moral
values.
Seeks to show, in the end, that despite their differences,
there is "a good deal of agreement" among the views of
Perry, Vivas, and Smith with respect to their respective
views of private and public morality; *laissez-faire*,
democratic social ethics; harmony in lieu of oversystemati-
zation of points of view; duty as the highest value; and a
"monistic" approach to morals.

I2   Miller, William David. "The Problem of Poetic Meaning and
       Value in the Aesthetics of Eliseo Vivas." Unpublished
       Doctoral Dissertation, the University of Iowa, 1971.
       105 pp.

     Argues that Vivas' notion of creation and discovery
allows the theorist to accommodate such radically divergent
critical approaches to literature as the mimetic, the formalistic, and the idealistic. Seeks to accommodate the
twin notions of the "intrinsic value" of poetry coupled
with the claim that poetry refers to meanings and values
that "subsist independently of that poetry." Contends
that "the failure to make this accommodation underlies the
schism between theory and practice of criticism, between
interpretation and evaluation, and forms the wide gulf
separating the schools of criticism today." Thus, "para-
doxical though Vivas' formulation be, I think we must
accept the fact that both creation and discovery are involved in the act which brings the poem into existence."
     Discusses, in turn, the aesthetic, the "ontic," the
critical, and the poetic problems that define Vivas'
aesthetics in an exposition that seeks to reveal Vivas'
"unique contributions" to the philosophy of art and to
enforce Vivas' repeated admonition to critics of the need
for "an adequate theoretical basis" for criticism. "Specifically, the critic who fails to deal adequately with the
theoretical basis underlying his normative statements, or
who adjures such statements altogether, can profit enormous-
ly from Vivas' account of objectivity in art."
     Provides an excellent study of the way Vivas' aesthetics
and critical theory are grounded on his axiological realism
(see also Curtler, F1; Jenkins, G22; Krieger, G26; and
Levy, G27) and provides an interesting example of how
Vivas' theory can be applied to criticism in such a way as
"to enable us to grasp Stevens [his case in point] in a way
that no simpler theory will permit." This exercise is
interesting because Vivas himself never devoted much attention to verse, and it generates the following tribute from
our author: "... before I had come to understand Vivas'
aesthetic principles, Stevens' verse was simply not available to me as experience...."

INDEX

Adams, Hazard, C67a
Adams, Nicholas B., D2
Adler, Mortimer, C113
Aesthetic Act, the C44
Aesthetic Judgment, C17
Aesthetic Response (Experience), C20, C21, C23, C29, C47, C79,
     C100, C109, C121 (see also Intransitive Apprehension)
Aiken, Henry, G1
Alexander, S., B1
Ambiguity of Poetry, C73, C95, C124 (see also Residential
     Function of Poetry)
Aristotle, C87 (see also Imitation)
Art, Place of, C14, C42, C44, C60, C70, C71, C109, C131
Autonomy of Art, C20, C43, C72, C84, C87, C90, G6
Autotelic, C16, C20 (see also Autonomy of Art)
Axiological Realism, A1, C62, C68, C71, C107, G1, I1 (see also
     Value)
Ayers, C.E., D39
Azorín (see Martínez Ruiz, José)

Babbitt, Irving, C36, C98
Barea, Arturo, D92
Barnes, Albert C., D54
Baroja, Pio, C1, D4, D10
Beardsley, Monroe, C74
Becker, Carl L., D53
Bell, Clive, B1
Bercovici, Konrad, D15
Bertocci, Angelo, C109, G2, G3, G4
Blasco Ibañez, Vicente, D20, D24
Boas, George, B1, D95
Bowra, C.M., C56
Bradley, A.C., B1, C64
Brennan, Joseph, G5
Brinton, Crane, D86
Brooks, Cleanth, D100

Vivas, Eliseo (Works) (cont.)
    "Philosophy for Nineteen Eighty-Four," C58
    "Philosophy of Control, The," C27
    "Philosophy of Culture, Aesthetics and Criticism: Some Prob-
        lems," C108
    "Pio Baroja y Nessi," C1
    "Poesia y Cultura," C136
    "'Poetry' and Philosophy," C123
    "Pragmatism and the Tragic Sense of Life," C133
    "Reality in Art," C21
    "Reality in Literature," C116
    "Recent Spanish Literature," C7
    "Reiterations and Second Thoughts on Cultural Relativism,"
        C89
    "Relativism: Its Paradoxes and Pitfalls," C91
    "Reply to Some Criticisms," C109
    Review of George P. Stein, *The Ways of Meaning in the Arts*,
        C120
    "Revolution in Personal Values, The," C94
    "Robinson Jeffers," C11
    "Science and the Studies of Man," C85
    "Self and Its Mask, The," C100
    "Semantics for Humanists, A," C72
    "Some Notes on Truth," C97
    "Spanish Heritage, The," C48
    "Substance of Tragedy, The," C96
    "Substance of *Women in Love*, The," C79
    "Symbols and Their Worlds," C137
    "Teachers and 'Teachers,'" C126
    "Theorists Without Theory," C55
    "Things and Persons," C101
    "Thoreau: The Paradox of Youth," C9
    "Tragedy and the Broader Consciousness," C119
    "Tragic Dimension, The," C81
    "Two Comments on Professor Graff's Essay," C135
    "Two Dimensions of Reality in *The Brothers Karamazov*, The,"
        C61
    "Two Lawrences, The," C78
    "Two Notes on the New Naturalism," C54
    "Unknown Critic, The," C3
    "Use of Art, The," C24
    "Value," C45
    "Value and Fact," C32
    "Was the Quest a Success?" C132
    "Were They Radicals or Intellectuals?" C106
    "What Is a Poem?" C71
    "Where Conquest Would Be Freedom," C2
    "Wisconsin's Experimental College," C13
    (see also under Vivas, Eliseo: Reviews; and under names of
        individual authors)

Lectures and Speeches
  "Aesthetics and the Theory of Signs," E4
  "Criticism, Intrinsic and Extrinsic," E3
  "Educated Man, The," E9
  "Function of Literature, The: Two Views and a Third," E5
  "Futility of Social Science, The," E1
  "Good Life for Modern Man, The," E2
  "Literature and Ideology," E6
  "Need for a Conservative Philosophy, The," E7
  "On Hofstader's 'Art and Knowledge,'" E10
  "On Moral Philosophy," E11
  "Universities Then and Now, The," E8
Reviews
  "About Modern Poetry," D45
  "Analysis of Renoir's Art," D54
  "Anti-Metaphysical Philosophy," D63
  "Art as Expression," D75
  "Bankrupt Realism," D61
  "Baroja Among Us," D10
  "Baruch or Benedictus," D47
  "Beauty as Quality," D71
  "Benavente as a Dramatist," D19
  "Buck Looks Back," D56
  "Chilean Mystic, A," D1
  "Conservative Testifies, A," D72
  "Critic of American Culture," D46
  "Critique of Santayana," D80
  "Dialectic According to Levy, The," D73
  "Entertaining Persiflage," D26
  "Error of Philosophy, The," D70
  "Essays After a 180 Degree Turn in Thought," D101
  "Evolutionary Aesthetics and Aristotle," D96
  "Ezra Pound," D48
  "For and Against the Founder," D97
  "Forerunner of Existentialism, A," D89
  "Francis Bacon," D44
  "Franz Kafka's Fine Writings," D90
  "From Prometheus to Maitreya," D85
  "From the Portuguese?" D27
  "Guedalla Facing South," D43
  "Heirlooms," D23
  "Historian of Our Stupidity," D32
  "Hyperindividualism," D76
  "Incoherent Nihilist," D103
  "Intellectualism in Vacuo," D37
  "Introduction to Dewey," D77
  "Jean-Jacques' Doctrines," D49
  "John Dewey's Humanism," D34